ENOUGH

ENOUGH

10 things
we should be telling
teenage girls

KATE CONNER

B&H
PUBLISHING GROUP
Nashville, Tennessee

978-1-4336-8293-3

Published by B&H Publishing Group
Nashville, Tennessee

Published in association with literary agent David
Van Diest of D.C. Jacobson & Associates, An Author
Management Company, www.dcjacobson.com.

Dewey Decimal Classification: 158
Subject Heading: GIRLS—COUNSELING
OF \ CHRISTIAN LIFE \ TEENAGERS—
COUNSELING OF

1 2 3 4 5 6 7 8 • 18 17 16 15 14

For the girl in all of us. You are enough.

And for Madeline, my sparkle.
I love you every single second.

Contents

Acknowledgments

David, Sarah, Jennifer, and Jana: A million thank yous for reading a million e-mails, editing a million drafts, and answering a million questions. So I guess three million thank yous. You are so, so good at what you do. You made everything better. I am blessed to have you on my team. Without you there would be no book.

My friends and family: whose names could fill another book. I am humbled by your friendship. You support, encourage, babysit, laugh, weep, and carry. You are my people. Without you there would be no book.

Jesus, You make me enough. Apart from You I have no good thing. All of this, and all of me, is from You, and through You, and to You.

Chapter 1

Neon Purple Leggings

"Style is a way to say who you
are without having to speak."
RACHEL ZOE

"Some people think luxury is the opposite of
poverty. It is not. It is the opposite of vulgarity."
COCO CHANEL

Fact: There is one involuntary, biochemical reflex genetically bred into every teenage girl on the planet. When the fearsome creature known as the teenage girl hears the word "modesty," she rolls her eyes and makes a guttural noise. A noise originating deep within the soul of the teenager and culminating in the throat: *"Ucgh."*

This noise is the perfect marriage between a scoff and a gag; the teenager has had twelve years to perfect it. She cannot help it—it's universal.

This is why it is so hard to talk to teenage girls about their clothing; you have to avoid the buzzwords. (Other buzzwords include "midriff" and "un-lady-like.")

Talking to a teenage girl about her wardrobe is like playing Taboo, that party game in which you have to describe an apple without using the words "computer," "iPod," "fruit," "red," "Mac," "pie," or "Snow White." The teenage girl functions as the buzzer; when she makes the "ucgh" noise, you're out.

But *modesty* is not a dirty word. It's not oppressive or archaic, and I've found that teenage girls aren't nearly as opposed to the concept of modesty as they are to the word itself.

Sometimes, in the name of real communication, you have to wade through all of the assumptions and preconceived notions, debunking and disarming as you go, before you can start talking about the stuff that matters.

The way women dress is one such opinion-laden, assumption-laden issue.

Three Realities

There are three realities that teenage girls need to understand before we can grab them by the proverbial (or literal) shoulders and shake some sense into them about their vapor-thin Hollister tank tops and the fact that they have to wear bras.

1. Women's bodies are beautiful. (Thank God, glory, hallelujah, amen.)
2. Men like to look at women.
3. It's not bad.

Women's bodies are beautiful.

Boys like breasts. As it turns out, they also like other various girl body parts including, but not limited to: stomachs, lips, hair, necks, thighs, calves, feet, hips, backs, shoulders, elbows, ear lobes, and pinky toes.

Boys aren't weird or creepy, they're just smart. Women's bodies are beautiful. One of the great perks of womanhood is that we get to be curvy and soft and inviting. Men are angular, muscular. And while that's nice enough, they're also hairy.

Femininity is a superpower.

Biologically speaking, adolescence is the time when this superpower emerges. Inconveniently enough, adolescence also places each newly christened superhero of a girl smack in the middle of the wondrous teenage phase of self-discovery.

I do not know what your teenage experience was like, but mine was magical. When I was fifteen I learned

that I was good at writing. When I was sixteen I learned
that I liked it. When I was thirteen I traveled to France.
I studied the language for eight more years and returned
after my college graduation, because the language and
culture never left me. I discovered my sense of humor
(Funny: hyperbole, puns, wit. Not funny: jokes involv-
ing any bodily function). I learned what kind of music I
liked; I discovered my spiritual gifts; I overcame chronic,
compulsive shyness; I spoke out about my faith; I fell in
love.

This kind of self-discovery and self-expression is
intoxicating and deliriously freeing.

Too often we make modesty about hiding.

"Cover that up."

"No one wants to see that."

"People will get the wrong idea about you."

"That looks trashy."

"You will not leave this house wearing that."

Just as girls are coming into their own, we issue
parental mandates that require them to conceal bits of
themselves that they are learning to love. Consequently,
"modesty" to a teenage girl feels a lot like someone trying to take away her superpower.

The first thing that young women need to understand about modesty is that hips and breasts are not
shameful body parts to be covered up or embarrassed
about. Hips and breasts (no matter how big or small)

are secret weapons of awesomeness, and it's okay to love them.

Men like to look at women.

Men like to look at women. Even married men. Even happily married men. Even good, kind, respectful, stand-up men. Even Christian men. Men are hardwired to enjoy women.

Says who?

Says God. Says the history of mankind, the animal kingdom, natural selection, the Bible, your pastor, and every teenage boy you'll ever meet. The fact that men are hardwired to enjoy women is a fact that pretty much everyone can agree on.

Women are beautiful and men like to look at them. The sooner we all reckon with this stone-cold reality, the sooner fifteen-year-old girls will stop using stupid non sequiturs like, "It's not my fault I have breasts. Therefore I have the right to buy a prom dress that is missing a torso." (Just why? Are they tanning at the prom? Jazzercising?)

Sound familiar? If not, it is because you have never been, had, met, or seen a teenage girl. You are likely a seventy-year-old man born at sea who has yet to find shore, because that one is straight out of their playbook.

A man's desire to look at a woman's body does not make him disrespectful; it makes him a man. It is just as unfair to say, "Every man who gapes at women is a creep," as it is to say, "Every woman who has big breasts is easy," or "Every girl who wears makeup is vain." It is categorically untrue.

I've noticed that we often make modesty about going on the defense—about protecting young women from predators. It doesn't take long for a bright girl to see the absurdity of this. A bright girl knows that a man who intends to stare will stare, regardless of what she is wearing. In the same vein, men who have committed not to stare, won't.

The notion that a woman can dress in a way that will prevent men from looking at her just doesn't hold water, not in the real world. This line of reasoning leads to burkas; "Maybe if I just cover up a little more . . ."

It also leads to spandex miniskirts; "If he's going to look anyway, then I might as well wear this."

Women's bodies are beautiful; modesty is not about hiding.

Men like to look at women; modesty is not about making oneself immune to stares.

It's not bad.

The fact that men are biologically hardwired to enjoy women's bodies is not bad. It's not primitive or dangerous. Men enjoying women's bodies is not perverted, gross, immature, or offensive.

When women get the idea in their heads that men are pigs because they like women's bodies, everything gets messed up. It causes hyper-antagonistic-feminists to hate men—to belittle and emasculate them. It causes hyper-conservatives to oppress women—insisting they cover up any body part that might interest a man, creating shame and frustration, even blaming women for their own harassment. On both ends of the very wide spectrum, when women discuss amongst themselves how gross men are, everybody loses.

Ladies, I'm about to make you blush, especially if your crusade against your teenager's wardrobe is motivated in large part by fear or protection. A man looking at your (and her) body and enjoying it is good. You want a man to look at your body and enjoy it.

If you think you don't, it's because you are only considering half of the equation. You think you don't want men to stare at you (or the teenage girl you love), but that's not true. You just don't want the *wrong* men to stare at you.

When the right man looks at you (to be clear, the right man is the man you marry), you walk a little taller, feel a little more beautiful. When my husband compliments my appearance, I feel secure in my relationship—secure in myself. A little piece of my soul lightens and sings, "I am beautiful! I am enough!" I do not feel uncomfortable because I'm in control. The day I married my husband I gave him the privilege of enjoying my superpower. He's here by invitation, and as such, his appreciation of me is welcome—and fun.

Modesty is not about making yourself homely or unattractive. Modesty and fashion are not mutually exclusive; neither are modest and beautiful.

Modesty is not about compensating for the poor behavior of men. It is impossible to make yourself immune to leering.

Modesty is not about feeling ashamed of breasts, hips, thighs, or any other beautiful, good, superpower body part.

Modesty is not the quenching of self-expression, the endorsement of conformity, or the oppression of femininity.

It's not hard to see why teenage girls buck so wildly at the idea of modesty when these are the things that come to mind at the mention of the word. No woman in her right mind would say, "Body issues, frustration, shame, ill-fitting clothes, and unattractiveness? Sign me up today!"

But if those are the things that modesty is not, then what is it?

Neon Purple Leggings

Teenage girls (and women everywhere) must come to terms with the fact that the way we look matters.

It's much warmer and fuzzier to say, "It's what's on the inside that counts." While that is absolutely true, it's not the whole story. The inside matters when you have to stand before God and answer for your life. The inside matters when you're determining your value and worth. The inside matters when you're looking for lasting beauty.

> Teenage girls (and women everywhere) must come to terms with the fact that the way we look matters. #10things

But the outside matters when you're looking for a job. It might not be fair, but it's true.

There isn't one of us that doesn't judge books by their covers all the time. You'll notice as you walk down the street that there are no cartoon caption bubbles hovering over people's heads that say things like, "I am wearing grease-stained yoga pants and my hair is matted in three or four places because I have four-month-old triplets, and I have not slept in four days," or "I just changed my own tire on the side of the road LIKE A BOSS. Please excuse the dirty fingernails."

(I'm glad that there is no caption bubble hovering over my head because 98 percent of the time it would say, "I have no excuse," or "I have totally let myself go.")

We don't get CliffsNotes on people; and we don't have time to get to know every person with whom we interact. You can blame the constraints of time and physics for that. When people make assumptions based strictly on physical appearance, it's not because they are shallow—it's because that is the only information they have to go on. These assumptions aren't character judgments (at least they shouldn't be), but inferences about a person's interests and style.

This makes the clothes you wear a walking advertisement for yourself. They are the closest thing you have to CliffsNotes, or a floating cartoon caption bubble.

Clothing speaks. It can say all sorts of things. It can say:

- My grandmother dressed me for Sunday school today. Do you like my pleated khakis?
- I spent too much money on this purse.
- I just came from working out, so I probably have my life together.
- I have a high-paying, white-collar job, as evidenced by my shiny shoes and power tie. Envy me!
- Check my tattered flannel shirt! I wish they'd bring back grunge.

- Hey, look at my breasts! Look at my breasts!
- I only listen to bands that nobody has ever heard of.
- I am obviously color-blind.
- I like animal prints more than average people do!
- I didn't feel like doing laundry this month.

Beneath all the pretense and protest and party lines of "I only dress for me," the truth is that people dress to identify with other people. Most of the time, clothes are either a reflection of what your teenager is, or what she is hoping to be. That's why preps dress like preps, hipsters dress like hipsters, and indie-boho-free-spirits dress like indie-boho-free-spirits.

Because clothing speaks, every person who dares venture outside of his or her own living room must ask themselves, "Is mine telling the truth?"

It is each teenage girl's responsibility to create an accurate image for herself, not the responsibility of the masses to interpret her correctly using their psychic powers.

The great thing about clothing speaking is that it can satisfy every drop of a young girl's need for self-expression; she can make her clothing say anything she wants. I've manipulated my clothing to say all sorts of things.

A few years ago I went shopping in New York City. I must have gotten caught up in the giant posters of fashion-forward women in neon clothing and giant, blown-out hair. In hindsight, the techno music was probably a contributing factor. Whatever the cause, I came home with a pair of neon purple leggings.

I am a stay-at-home mom. My husband is a pastor. If I leave the house (a big "if"), it is to go to church with lots of little old ladies. I don't know what I thought I was going to do with neon purple leggings, but they seemed very important at the time. I owned those neon purple leggings for an entire year and never wore them once. I would see them lying there in my sock drawer; I would touch them fondly, my fashion-forward neon purple leggings, then close the drawer and pull on my jeans.

The following year, we moved to Alabama—not exactly fashion-forward neon purple leggings territory. On the very first Sunday we were there, I touched my fashion-forward neon purple leggings thoughtfully. It was first impression time, and in a moment of extraordinary courage I decided, "For all these people know, I am the hippest of young mothers and I come from a place where people wear neon purple leggings all the time." Then I said, "Let there be style!" and I marched into church in my neon purple leggings where people seriously regretted having hired us to come there.

No, but they did say, "You are so stylish, I could never pull that off."

I used my clothing to make a statement about myself. And now, I can wear anything I please and nobody is ever surprised, because in their minds I will always be "the kind of girl who can wear neon purple leggings."

Modesty is about dressing on purpose. It is about being mature enough to reckon with some realities: the reality that men like to look at women; the reality that if a girl displays her breasts overtly, men will stare, no matter how great of guys they are; the reality that clothing speaks and that the way we look matters.

Modesty is about choosing clothes that intentionally communicate what you want the world to know about yourself; it is an integral part of creating your own, truthful image—the very thing all teenage girls are trying so desperately to do.

> Modesty is about choosing clothes that intentionally communicate what you want the world to know about yourself. #10things

Basic Marketing

I mentioned how mutually delightful it is when a man can enjoy his wife visually. It's flattering. In the words of Carole King, "You make me feel like a natural woman."[1] When the right man looks at your body, you feel affirmed.

13

Since wrong is the polar opposite of right, it stands to reason that when the wrong man looks at your body, you feel the polar opposite of affirmed. You feel degraded.

When the right man enjoys your feminine super-power, he is there by invitation. You are in control and every action, right down to each stolen glance, is based upon mutual trust and respect. You are a whole person that is loved.

When the wrong man enjoys your body, it is a violation. When a man on the street leers, catcalls, smirks and nods his head, whispers to his buddies, or makes a crude gesture, it is reprehensible; he is not invited. His staring makes you feel as naked as he is imagining you to be, and the mixture of anger, embarrassment, and disgust twists and burns in your stomach. You are not a whole person that is loved; you are parts that have been objectified. And let us not come to this issue with platitudes about men admiring God's creation. I know how it feels to be noticed by men, and I know how it feels to be objectified. There is a discernable difference in both the behavior and in the way it makes me feel. I have to believe that we all know the difference. I refuse to shame the noticing and, just as vehemently, I refuse to tolerate the objectifying.

Modesty is about taking control. Dressing modestly is a way of telling every man in the world, "I have not given you permission to stare at my breasts. That privilege belongs to a man who knows me—my personality, my handwriting, my family, my stories—my whole self. I am not a Playboy bunny; I do not exist for the entertainment of men. I am more than that, so you don't get to use me that way, even in passing."

For your teenager, dressing modestly is about harnessing her superpower—taking control.

Let me be clear, women who dress provocatively do not deserve to be disrespected, degraded, or violated in any way. Ever. A woman in the buff is still not "asking for it." But if a woman dresses provocatively and does not relish the attention her body garners from men, she is not telling the truth with her clothing. There is a breakdown in communication, a disconnect.

This is basic marketing—PR, reputation management. We are all our own agents, and teenage girls need to learn to represent themselves well. If they don't mind being viewed as sex objects without thoughts, feelings, or skills outside of the bedroom, then by all means, they should dress to call attention to their sex organs. I can't fault that logic, it is at least consistent. But if your teenage girl wants to be known for her great ideas or her cross-country running accomplishments, she has to put those things in the display case. The same principle applies to us. If we would be known for our business savvy, we must display our business savvy more prominently than our great rear ends in pencil skirts so tight they could split. (I say more prominently because I do love a good pencil skirt.)

While there is no body part you can accentuate with a good belt to communicate business savvy, you can ensure that the passerby isn't allowed to enjoy your breasts until he's gotten to know all about your business savvy, among other things.

If your teenage girl wants to be known for her humor, her kindness, her eyes, her thoughts on social issues, her athleticism, or her confidence, she must put those things on display more prominently than her breasts.

Yes, her body is beautiful, but she is more than a body. What a shame it would be if she made it so easy for people to ignore the rest of her.

Modesty allows people to see the rest of her—to see the best of her.

Modesty allows people to see the rest of her—to see the best of her. #10things

On Attracting Men

I work with teenage girls every single day. I don't have enough fingers and toes to count how many times a young lady has come to me, baffled and disillusioned, plopped down on my couch and said, *"I only attract jerks."* ("Jerks" is interchangeable with "creeps," "idiots," and other, more colorful terms.)

My response is always the same: "Every woman attracts a handful of creeps in her lifetime. You're not broken; it just means you're a beautiful girl. But (every momma, grandmomma, and youth leader knows there is a "but") if you are *only* attracting creeps, there might be something to discuss."

Then I drop the bomb.

"If the guys who want to date you leave as soon as they get what they want, if they don't make any effort to get to know what you're thinking and feeling, if they are constantly trying to put their hands on your body, or if they seem too interested in the bodies of other women—if you notice a long line of losers, you have to ask yourself, *What am I doing that is causing these creeps to flock?*"

This is almost always met with stunned silence as the teenager tries to decide whether or not I've offended her. I proceed quickly before the "ucgh" reflex kicks in and she's gone forever.

"The truth is that, by and large, you'll attract what you bait. Are you carrying yourself to bait godly young men? Or boys that sexualize everything?"

Looks of horror. Teenagers don't know what to do with themselves when grown-ups say things like "sexualize." It really freaks them out. (You'll notice that this is the point in the conversation when girls start tugging at their tank tops to cover up their cleavage.)

We are getting back to the very basics of math—back to common sense and the most primal laws of attraction.

Men who value compassion are drawn to compassionate women. Men who value intelligence are drawn to intelligent women. Men who value style are drawn to stylish women. Men who value bacon are drawn to women who cook bacon. There is a pattern here.

If a teenage girl wants to date a godly man, she should endeavor to be the godly woman he is seeking.

If her figure outshines her positivity and personality as the most prominent thing about her, then she is baiting the kind of boy whose primary interest is what is under her shirt and how easily he can access it.

Are the girls you love baiting the kind of men you would wish for them?

The other issue at hand is that when young women display their bodies without much reservation, they are shutting down all the male brains in the vicinity. Studies show that sex (and related matter) turns off higher brain functions in men; they start thinking with their hormones, if you will. This is precisely why the same women who insist on dressing scantily are the ones complaining about what mindless brutes men are.

A 2008 Princeton University study, originally published in the *Journal of Cognitive Neuroscience*, revealed that when men viewed images of bikini-clad women, the part of their brains associated with tools and the intention to commit action lit up.[2] There was also a remarkable inactivity in the part of the brain that processes another person's thoughts and feelings. No human interaction and a desire to use and act upon—this is the very definition of objectification. A supplementary study revealed that men associated images of women in bikinis with first-person verbs like "I handle. I push. I grab." The same men associated pictures of women dressed in casual business attire with third-person verbs: "She handles. She pushes. She grabs." In one scenario, the women were out of control (being acted upon), and in the other the women were in control (the ones doing the acting).

It is so important to note that this isn't bad. These findings don't indicate that men are flawed or innately disrespectful. They simply reveal information about the (God-created and "very good") male brain. The takeaway is that if we, as women, want to be viewed as whole people, we must present ourselves as whole people. The logical conclusion is that, because there appears to be some hardwiring that makes it difficult for men to engage a sexily dressed woman on a deeper level, we should dress in a way that allows us to be taken seriously. Keep sex-brain out of the workplace and, for crying out loud, out of high schools.

> *If we, as women, want to be viewed as whole people, we must present ourselves as whole people. #10things*

This is relevant to your teenagers because if a young lady desires a meaningful relationship—if she wants a boy to value qualities in her besides her cup size—she'll need his higher brain function intact. In other words, she should put on some more clothes so that she can engage the opposite sex on a higher brain wave. Everybody wins.

The Crux of the Matter: The Heart

I fear that up until this point, I may have oversimplified the matter. Everything I've written is practical, tried, and true, but it's also operating on a dangerous assumption.

It is operating on the assumption that smart, bright young women do not wish to be thought of as sex objects. But the sticky thing is, some do. Some young women have been seduced by the power of it. They relish the ability to turn a man's brain to mush. They delight in wielding their superpower over the first boy who comes close enough to be manipulated—flattered and validated by the knowledge that they can flash a little skin and get anything they want. There is no talking a girl out of immodesty if immodesty is her goal.

This is a sin-sick heart problem, and it cannot be remedied by logic.

When C. S. Lewis reflected on our sin-sick heart problems, he wrote, "It would seem that Our Lord finds our desires not too strong, but too weak. . . . We are far too easily pleased."[3]

This is simply, exactly, correct. The part of a woman's heart that seeks to be found beautiful has been twisted and perverted into a desperate desire for attention. And yet, it is not that teenage girls desire attention too much, it is that they do not desire that which is greater: respect.

All attention is not equal. It is possible to get a man's attention and never have his respect.

No woman can revel in the attention her breasts elicit from men, and then be offended that her breasts are all that men are interested in. She wanted attention, and she got it.

No woman can delight in men's drooling, be flattered by their stammering, manipulate them with her miniskirt, and then be surprised when her body is the only thing they care about. She wanted attention, and she got it.

No woman should settle for the ability to make a man drool when instead she could have his admiration.

Dear sisters, all attention is not equal. Your teenage girl thinks she wants attention, but she doesn't. She wants respect.

Teach her to use modesty as a tool to pursue that which is greater: admiration, respect, and love.

Chapter 2

The Tanning ~~Bed~~ Trap

"In 1,000 years, archaeologists
will find tanning beds and think that
we fried people as punishment."[1]

I am not just Irish, I am super-Irish.

My name is Kathryn Elizabeth. I have freckles and auburn hair. My grandparents lived in Dublin for thirty years; my mother went to high school there, and I had already visited by the time I was three. I have tea almost every day; I love potatoes and U2; I grew up listening to Makem and Clancy and watching a Riverdance VHS tape. I know all the words to "Danny Boy," "The Fox," "Wild Rover," "Mary Mack," and "All God's Creatures Got a Place in the Choir."

Do you know what this means? This means that I will never have a tan as long as I live.

This means that as a child, while all my friends were plunging their bronzed bikini-ed bodies into the ocean, I was getting slathered with SPF 50—under my T-shirt.

This means that my cheeks are ruddy seven days a week, and that when I get hot, they turn so bright and blotchy it looks like somebody crushed slices of ripe watermelon on them.

It means that when I was in the eighth grade and decided to lighten my hair with lemon juice and peroxide, it turned bright, brassy orange, and my cheeks were ruddy with embarrassment for months. (Do not EVER, even under threat of violence, allow your daughter to do this. That tidbit is free, you're welcome.)

It means that my skin is so fair you can see my hair straight through it. It means that I could shave three times today and still have a million dark speckles up and down my legs from hairs that will grow tomorrow.

It means that in the winter months I cannot find makeup light enough. "Porcelain Ivory," which is the fairest shade available at the drugstore, is too dark. (A friend once suggested Wite-Out. It's worth a shot.)

It means that when I was in the sixth grade I started hating my skin—and felt shame about it for the next nine years.

I was in the eleventh grade the first time I set foot into a tanning bed. (This was after several self-tanning creams gone awry—and by awry, I mean orange, streaky, and more than a little conspicuous around the ankles.)

The experience was a pale girl's worst nightmare (besides, of course, staying pale forever). The salon was manned by a petite lady with skin the color of burnt sienna, and the whole place smelled like a coconut stuffed inside a sweaty sock. There was a case full of lotions up front: accelerators, calming creams, and mystery products, all in opaque bottles featuring pictures of neon parrots.

The lady asked me if I'd ever been tanning before, and when I said no, I had to sign a waiver.

Note: Any activity that requires you to sign a waiver probably isn't the safest.

After I agreed not to sue her family if I got cancer, the lady asked me how long I'd like to tan. I was unprepared for this question. I stared at her blankly.

"Most people go in for eleven or twelve minutes the first time," she offered after an uncomfortable silence.

"Maybe six then," I whispered.

She rolled her eyes and pulled a pair of goggles out of a canister of blue juice—the same, supposedly sanitary, blue juice that the combs sit in at the hair salon. She told me that the bed would turn on automatically in two minutes.

Two minutes?!

I galloped awkwardly down the hall, strapping the moist goggles to my head as I went—I didn't want to get cancer and be blind. They were so tight that they suctioned themselves to my eye sockets with a loud *schlooop*! Everything went black and began to spin. Here I faced a critical decision: keep the goggles on and fumble around in the blackness trying to undress myself? Or take off the goggles, undress, and hopefully replace them before ultraviolet rays burned out my retinas?

And speaking of undressing—what degree of undress is appropriate in this situation? I didn't bring a bathing suit—that seemed like a rookie mistake. And though I was so obviously a tanning novice, I was determined not to look like one. Spoiler alert: too late.

I decided to take off the goggles.

Once the blood started flowing to my brain again, I noticed a small pile of towels and a spray bottle full of more blue juice.[2] I deduced that this was for sanitizing the bed. Here I faced a second critical decision: sanitize the bed before putting the goggles on—was there time for this? Or lay my delicate, bare, Irish skin onto a surface where another person's skin had previously lain—sweating. Or put the goggles on first, and try to stay upright long enough to sanitize the bed, which would likely result in my passing out on the ground, naked, with one arm in the tanning bed holding a spray bottle and badly burned.

I sensed that my two minutes were almost up; the pressure was mounting. I was still fully clothed, holding the spray bottle in one hand and the death goggles in the other. Time was running out! I felt like a member of a bomb squad faced with an impossible task and T-minus thirty seconds to detonation. I panicked. I whipped off my shirt, clenched my eyes shut, and started spritzing furiously. Then I spiked the bottle, grabbed a towel, and swiped at the bed blindly, mopping off what I could while trying to simultaneously unbutton my jeans.

You guys, I'm such a professional.

I decided to leave my undergarments on, mostly because I was in too desperate a state to consider the alternative; I did not have the mental energy to make that kind of decision. I suctioned the goggles back to my head and slid my leg onto the bed just as the lights buzzed to life. Close call.

Then my elbow found a puddle of unmopped juice and I landed clumsily into full tanning position with an ungraceful thud.

Okay, so far so good.

Another thing nobody thought to mention is that there is a time-space continuum thing happening inside of tanning beds. You know how God says that a thousand years are like a day to Him and a day is like a thousand years? I think God was in a tanning bed when He said that, because one tanning-bed-minute feels like at least one thousand real-life minutes. A six-minute stay in a tanning bed feels like an eternity lost in the Sahara.

I didn't breathe for the first minute, which felt like an hour.

During the second minute I exhaled.

During the third minute I peeped my eyes open. The skin around them was so puffed up from the goggles that I couldn't see properly. Everything looked distorted— blue and ethereal. I thought, *This must be what it looks like when people get abducted by aliens.*

During the fourth minute I thought, *It's actually quite nice in here—warm, relaxing. Ahhhhhh. I'm going to look like a Greek goddess when I get out of this thing, which should be any minute now.*

During the fifth minute I thought, *It has definitely been longer than six minutes. Oh, no. She forgot about me. I don't know where the off-switch is! And I can't find it with these blasted goggles on my face! Oh Jesus. Jesus, I love You; please turn it off, please turn it off, please turn it off, please turn it off.*

During the sixth minute I thought, *I am going to die in here! How is it legal for something to get this hot? I am dehydrated! I am burned! My skin! My retinas! HELP!!!*

*And for the love of all the kittens, WHAT IS WRONG
WITH THESE GOGGLES!?!?!*

Then the tanning bed clicked off.

I climbed out, stunned, sweaty, and cheeks ruddier
than they had ever been. I sanitized the bed as a cour-
tesy, put my clothes back on, and left—smelling a little
like a coconut stuffed inside a sweaty sock.

———

You would think that after such a traumatic inaugu-
ral experience that my first trip to the tanning bed would
have been my last. I'm sorry to say that it was not.

I tanned only very occasionally through high school:
a week before each dance and one before summer. I
took it easy mostly because my mom took to leaving
pamphlets about melanoma on my pillow. So subtle. The
first time she did it, I walked into my bedroom, picked
up the brochure, and curled my lip in disgust when I saw
rotted-looking black spots on an old man's arm.

"What is this?" I asked her.

"Oh, I just saw it at work and thought it was interesting. Did you know that sun damage is cumulative? That
even though a burn goes away the damage never does?
That every sunburn you get builds on the one before
it? Did you know that one bad burn can do irreparable
damage to your skin? Did you????"

"Uh . . . no. But now I do. Thanks, Mom. Do you, uh, want these pictures back?"

"No, you can keep them," she chirped.

"Whatever."

"I don't tan often," I reasoned to myself every time I went. "And I don't use any weird lotions or lay out for hours."

If you know a teenage girl who tans, she'll say these things too. She may even have excuses that weren't available to me, like, "I never burn. I don't need sunscreen. I have naturally tan skin. My grandparents were fill-in-the-blank-with-some-sun-tolerant-ethnicity." (Just rub it in my face, why don't you.) She'll also say that it clears up her skin (which is true), and that it will keep her from getting burned during her first pool trips of the summer. (You know what else does that? Sunscreen.)

My most habitual tanning happened during my freshmen year of college. That year, my friend, Nicole, discovered Kitty's. "Kitty's Hair and Tanning" was a dingy building in a gravel parking lot, twelve miles from campus. That we willingly set foot into that place is our everlasting shame. Kitty was a leathery woman dressed in pink with an impressive Jeri curl perched on top of her head—she probably owned stock in Aqua-Net.

Kitty had four tanning beds in the back of her one-room salon ("salon" is a generous word), presumably from the eighties, just like the curling, yellowed posters on the walls. Kitty charged two dollars per session.

Nicole and I were broke college students with no mothers to leave melanoma pamphlets on our pillows—and we were sold. For three months I tanned recreationally—almost every day. I grew accustomed to the tanning ritual (I even learned how to work the goggles), and the more my tanning-savvy grew, the more I was convinced that no trip to the tanning bed would ever be as traumatic as my first.

I was wrong.

One day, Nicole and I headed to Kitty's after class for an afternoon tanning session. We pulled off the rural highway to find the gravel parking lot deserted. We walked to the door and were surprised to find it cracked. We stuck our noses inside to find an old man inside sweeping up hair; he looked like he could be homeless. When he saw us craning our necks through the crack in the door, he told us that Kitty had left early and that he was just locking up.

Now, if you want proof that tanning kills brain cells, here's your ammunition: when this strange, homeless-looking man offered to let us tan, alone in the building after hours, we said yes.

It was not until I was scantily clad and trapped inside a giant glowing bed that I thought, *Who was that guy? I've never seen him around before. He could lock the doors!*

*He could be coming in here right now! He could be walking
in on Nicole right now! Nobody will ever hear us scream!*

I held my breath, listening, and looking for anything
with which I could inflict physical harm. I decided that
the big fan standing in the corner was my best shot. Blunt-
force trauma. When my bed clicked off, I dressed hurriedly,
grabbed my keys (shoved between my fingers, poised to jab
eyeballs), and Nic and I booked it out of there.

On the way home, Nicole told me that while I was
thinking about how to rescue her, she was thinking
about how to rescue me. She told me that her weapon of
choice would have been the curling irons that stay heated
up in their little holders (so much better than my fan
plan). That is friendship. When you find a friend willing
to run naked out of a tanning bed and stab an old man
with a hot curling iron for you—you keep her.

———

After two semesters' worth of textbooks, pizza, and
ill-advised trips to Kitty's, I was flat broke. Tanning lost
some of its allure—due mostly to my extreme poverty
and crippling guilt.

Providentially, it was at precisely this time that God
introduced me to Leslie—a woman to whom I am forever indebted. It was Leslie who taught me about The
Beauty Trap.

The Beauty Trap

I was sitting on a cold, tile floor with seventy other girls from my dorm when everything I ever thought about my skin (and my weight) changed forever.

Leslie, the woman who would become my mentor for the remainder of the semester, said, "I've heard a thousand and one self-esteem messages in my life, and none of them has had much impact on my self-esteem. That's why this is not a self-esteem message. I want to show you how I know that beauty is a trap."

Then, together, we looked through the annals of history.

During the Middle Ages, the masses labored outdoors all day, just to survive. They worked to grow food, collect water, and maintain the land of their feudal lords. Women labored strenuously and had precious little food; they were thin. Women worked outdoors as long as it was daylight; they were dark. And when you flip through a textbook or stroll through an art museum you'll notice that the standard for beauty during the Middle Ages was a thick—even overweight—woman; the fairer the better. It represented wealth. The most elusive body type, the one nearly impossible to attain under the circumstances of the day, was beautiful.

In stark contrast to the Middle Ages stands America today. The American masses work sedentary jobs, all indoors. We work in offices and cubicles, virtually chained to computer monitors all day long. We leave for work before the sun is up and return after it's set. Our food-cooking, clothes-washing machines (for which I'm very grateful) make hard physical labor all but obsolete. We have an abundance of food—of cheap, convenient, unhealthy food. On any given night we can choose: Mexican? Chinese? Thai? Indian? Italian? American? French? German? Moroccan? We live in a technologically dependent, drive-through world. And when you turn on the television, behold! Our standard for beauty is a dis-proportionally thin woman; the tanner the better. The most elusive body type, nearly impossible to attain under the circumstances of the day, is beautiful.

It was the same in every culture, in every era. I couldn't believe it.

It was like my whole life I'd been looking at the issue of "beauty" through a peephole. I knew that the indus-try today was a trap; I knew that women with straight hair wanted curly hair and women with curly hair wanted straight hair. I knew that shapely girls wanted to be thin and that thin girls wanted breasts so badly they could die. But as Leslie walked us through history that night, it was like someone swung the whole door wide open. Suddenly, I wasn't just looking at *my* body, *my* skin, *my* self-esteem; suddenly I could hear the collective yearning of every woman in history who ever spent her life chasing after an ideal that was a setup from the start.

Suddenly, I was mad.

This trap—this cruel, sadistic trap—is why fair, freckled girls give themselves sun poisoning and blisters and cancer to be tan, and think they're getting a good deal. This evil trap is why dark girls bleach their skin trying to pass the lingering standard of the "brown paper bag test" and assume that it just comes with the territory. It's why half of the cosmetic surgeries out there are to make women thinner and the other half are to put a little more junk into women's proverbial trunks.

It's ludicrous! It's senseless that we can find beauty in literally every type of women, but can't for the life of us find it in ourselves.

And Satan laughs at our dissatisfaction. He smacks his lips, laps it up, and revels in it. I hate him. I hate Satan for causing pain, but even more for enjoying it. If I'm not careful, I sometimes find myself thinking that Satan is just doing his job, fulfilling his cosmic role. I imagine him as an actor cast to play the villain—just an archetype. But he is the villain. He connives to orchestrate our destruction; he mocks our inner aching, our jealousy, and our self-harm. I hate him.

> *It's senseless that we can find beauty in literally every type of women, but can't for the life of us find it in ourselves. #10things*

I refuse to be a victim of the beauty trap; you will not find me among its casualties.

I refuse to tan because, why should I have to be tan? Because I want to? This begs the question why I want to. Because it's beautiful? Well, so is fair. I reject the notion that what I am not is more beautiful than what I am. I believe in health. I believe in caring for my body well. I will not ignore weight that I should lose under the pretense of embracing self-esteem. I believe in exercise, good food choices, and hygiene. I believe in fashion, style, and makeup. I believe in making the most of what I've got. But I think that as a human race we've got it all wrong. I believe God thought up beauty and splashed it all over creation and humankind for us to enjoy. I believe it's not nearly as narrow or elusive as we've been conditioned to believe. And above all else, I believe that as the creator of beauty, God must know the truth about it, and I rest in the fact that what He tells me about beauty is not a snare, but a healing balm.

> *I reject the notion that what I am not is more beautiful than what I am. #10things*

The king is enthralled by your beauty; honor him, for he is your lord. (Ps. 45:11)

All beautiful you are, my darling; there is no flaw in you. (Song of Sol. 4:7)

For you created my inmost being; you knit me together in my mother's womb. I praise you because I am fearfully and wonderfully made; your works are wonderful, I know that full well. My frame was not hidden from you when I was made in the secret place, when I was woven together in the depths of the earth. Your eyes saw my unformed body; all the days ordained for me were written in your book before one of them came to be. (Ps. 139:13–16)

"The LORD does not look at the things man looks at. Man looks at the outward appearance, but the LORD looks at the heart." (1 Sam. 16:7)

Charm is deceptive, and beauty is fleeting; but a woman who fears the LORD is to be praised. (Prov. 31:30)

The perfect shade of skin for you is the one you have. The perfect body frame is the one you've got. Real beauty doesn't trap you, it frees you. Real beauty doesn't make you die inside, it makes you come alive.

Enough

Even when we hear the real, God-truth about beauty, we tend to let it roll off our backs because we think we have to really believe it before we can act on it. But that's not true; that's upside down. We can practice body-love before we actually love our bodies. We can practice contentment. We can practice Enough.

Practice it on days that you feel so frumpy and icky that you cannot even recognize the woman in the mirror. Practice it on the hardest days, the days that you don't believe it; that's when you need it. Practice Enough so that your daughter can too. Teach her how to love a body that's grown babies, and still bears the evidences of children having lived on the inside. Teach your teenager that your yoga pants are your uniform, that they are a sign of expertise, which is quite the opposite of letting oneself go.

Exercise and love yourself.

Eat well and love yourself.

Have dessert and love yourself.

Brush your hair (or don't) and love yourself.

Don your ever-loving yoga pants and LOVE YOURSELF.

Contentment is hard, and hard things take practice. So practice. Dig down deep and daily-do.

For me, practicing contentment looks like taking care of my fair skin. For me, it looks like not tanning, like wearing sunscreen, like loving my freckles. And I do, I love them. For me it looks like doing jumping jacks every time I change a diaper. It looks like having family dinners when I can manage it—and refusing to carry guilt when I can't.

For me it looks like telling my daughter about how I learned to love my nose, even though I wanted a nose job until

> Contentment is hard, and hard things take practice. So practice. #10things

I was twenty. It looks like letting Jesus be the magnet inside that makes people want to draw near. It looks like cultivating a tender heart and an iron backbone. It means kind words: kind words to others, about others, to me, about me. Kind words in my head about my mommy-pouch, or under-belly, or whatever you call that abdominal remnant of childbearing that we still carry. Kind words about my skin. Kind words about the dark hair on my fair arms.

Don't lose yourself over the impossible ideal. Climb up out of the beauty trap and just be. Be you, and pretty, and content, and free.

Yes, be free.

Chapter 3

In the Cafeteria with a Megaphone

"If you are not kind on the Internet,
then you're not kind."
GLENNON MELTON

Before 2007, teenage girls were not allowed on Facebook.

It was a simpler time.

If a teenage girl wanted to bemoan the loss of a two-month texting relationship with a boy from her homeroom class, she had to find a group of friends willing to listen to her self-involved melodrama.

If she wanted to win allies in the battle against her parents, she had to explain how backwards and unaware her parents were to each friend individually. It took much longer to amass forces.

If she wanted to passive-aggressively confront a friend about said friend's behavior, she had to get creative about it. The preferred method was to write a fake note to a mutual friend and leave it in a place where the offending friend would find it and thereby deduce that all her friends were talking about her behind her back. Teenage girls had to be a lot smarter before 2007.

Today, Facebook offers teenage girls the luxury of whining, complaining, arguing, gossiping, attention-seeking, and passive-aggressively attacking their friends and exes with the click of a mouse.

Facebook is a master at getting teenage girls to open up—a real conversational wizard. It asks, caringly, "What's on your mind?"

Prompted by such sincere interest, teenage girls tell Facebook anything. They tell Facebook things they wouldn't dare tell their parents, their friends, or their hairdressers.

They fill in the box dutifully.

Gratefully.

Much too honestly.

Then, because they're feeling all empowered and validated, they click "Share!"

Et voilà. Their most private thoughts in black and white before their eyes. It is official. They are heard.

Facebook gives us humans something we've always wanted—something we crave: a captive audience.

Facebook always listens. Facebook doesn't judge us. Facebook hears where we're coming from. Facebook knows how smart we are. How mature we are. How unappreciated we are. How right we are.

Facebook is a dream-come-true in that way. The days of venting in front of mirrors, imagining what it would be like to really let someone have it are over. No more scenarios played out in heads, no more dreaming up how sorry someone would be if they could see your teenager crying in her bedroom. Facebook makes all of this irrelevant. Now your teenager can just tell everyone that she is crying in her bedroom.

In 2007, Facebook opened itself up to the general public, allowing every teenage girl to type up what she was feeling to no one in particular. The great irony is that what she writes to no one can be seen by everyone.

And thus, the age of oversharing was born.

Anonymity

There is an Internet lie out there making its rounds and sinking its teeth into the minds of teenagers and adults alike. The lie is this:

"If it's anonymous, it doesn't count."

If nobody knows who I'm talking about, no harm done.

If nobody knows it was I who said it, there can be no consequences.

If I don't name names, it's not gossip.

> *Words are swords. They can be used powerfully for good or evil and they have the ability to cut us to the quick. #10things*

Each of these is categorically untrue. We embrace them to appease our consciences. They are lies we live with to justify our rampant oversharing.

First of all, words are swords. They can be used powerfully for good or evil and they have the ability to cut us to the quick. It doesn't matter if you can't see who's wielding the sword—it cuts you just the same. Anonymous swords can still make you bleed.

And second, the Internet is not anonymous.

I cannot count on hands and feet the number of Facebook statuses I've read from teenage girls that sound something like this:

> "I hate how these girls are all talk and then when you go confront them about it they wanna back down and try to be all innocent when you know the truth."

> "You will never know how I feel because I will never tell you. I can't trust you enough to tell you

what I feel without you putting me down and hurting me. So I'd rather just feel alone."

"Tired of guys playing games. If you did it then tell me! Don't lie! Because there is NO reason for it. You're just stupid by even doing that. You're a jerk, don't talk to me anymore if you're going to pull that stuff."

"When you know someone for almost two years and they turn on you and lie to you but they want YOU to tell the truth and you do. I'm done with stuck-up people these days."

"If they wanna talk to me they know how to reach me. I'm done texting people to be ignored."[1]

There is nothing more juvenile than an emotional, passive-aggressive accusation directed at a peer whose identity is so thinly veiled that an orangutan could figure it out.

The people who can read a teenage girl's Facebook status are the people she has added as her Facebook "friends."[2] And do you know who she has added as her "friends"? HER FRIENDS. When a teenage girl posts a status update, her friends from school, band, sports teams, church, work, and the neighborhood read it. Therefore, a passive-aggressive Facebook status from your teenage girl is essentially the same thing as you sending a mass e-mail to everyone in your address book that says, "I hate it when *some husbands* leave coffee grounds all over the floor. Come on, you're a grown man."

Can you see the ludicrousness?

Teenage girls have a hard time wrapping their minds around this; they don't understand why it's such a big deal because the Internet and everyone on it has very bad manners. It is as if the commonly accepted social rules don't apply on the Internet, even though the people there are still subject to social hurts. Social media is not its own separate world anymore; it is a real part of life—an integral part of the way we interact with other people. Our girls need to understand that posting a Facebook status that references another person accomplishes the same thing as standing up on a table in the cafeteria with a megaphone and announcing, *"I hate it when CERTAIN PEOPLE (cough, cough) don't text me back!"*

And she does all this while shooting daggers at the culprit. Ninety percent of those in earshot would know exactly to whom your teenager is referring. The rest are so engrossed in their rectangular cafeteria pizza that the chemistry teacher could streak through the room in nothing but a lab coat and they would just keep plucking off the little pepperoni cubes. They are classmates! Mutual friends. None of them are so dense that they cannot deduce from their knowledge of social politics who the offending non-texter-backer is.

A Facebook status like this accomplishes the following:

1. It makes your teenager look sullen and pouty.
2. It makes your teenager look immature and self-involved.
3. It makes those who know to whom your teenager is referring make unfair judgments about the non-texter-backer.
4. It makes the non-texter-backer mad, hurt, offended, and embarrassed.
5. It gives the non-texter-backer a reason to hold a grudge, or retaliate via Facebook message/cafeteria megaphone.

In no real-life situation is this kind of public denouncement of another person acceptable, but the false sense of anonymity granted by Facebook makes it fair game for teenagers today. The result is drama on a cosmic scale.

You would do well to remind your teenager that she is not a Navaho wind talker. People are, shockingly, capable of cracking her super-duper secret code. Remind her that people over the age of six can read between the lines, and that words, like swords, have no regard for anonymity. Anonymous swords wielded by anonymous foes slice hearts and friendships into broken, bleeding pieces. Exhort her to use her Facebook statuses not as instruments of wickedness, but as instruments of grace.

Do not offer the parts of your body to sin, as instruments of wickedness, but rather offer yourselves to God, as those who have been brought from death to life; and offer the parts of your body to him as instruments of righteousness. For sin shall not be your master, because you are not under law, but under grace. (Rom. 6:13–14)

Every username, every avatar, gravatar, Twitter handle, and profile picture is a real person with real feelings. Just because you interact with them through a monitor doesn't remove the imperative to be nice. I love how Glennon Melton said it: "If you are not kind on the Internet, then you're not kind."[3]

> Anonymous swords wielded by anonymous foes slice hearts and friendships into broken, bleeding pieces. #10things

Inconvenient Truths: Internet Edition

At some point, your teenage girl will probably tell you that you just don't understand how fill-in-the-blank social media works. She will say, "I don't use it that way," or "Mom, nobody does that," or "It's not a big deal." All of that is probably true, sorry. But there are also some things that your socially superior, tech-savvy teenager doesn't know about the Internet. I call them "inconvenient Internet truths."

- Employers check their employees' Facebook and Twitter accounts.
- They also screen job applicants this way.
- If a girl has wild spring break photos, twenty-first-birthday photos, or her status updates are dramatic and irresponsible, she is unlikely to get a job.
- Contrary to what most teenagers think, this is not unfair. Nobody is discriminating against anybody; employers are guarding their businesses and brands, which is well within their right to do. Nobody is in trouble for celebrating; they are in trouble for thoughtlessly parading irresponsible celebrations on the Internet.
- Parents check Facebook.
- Boyfriends' parents check Facebook.
- Things that other people post about you can be as much of a liability as things you post yourself.
- A lot of people lose their jobs because of things they post on personal blogs. This is perfectly legal.

- If you post something on the Internet, it is no longer private; privacy is no longer a reasonable expectation.
- Internet surfing leaves a trail.
- People misrepresent themselves on the Internet all the time, in hundreds of different ways.
- Strangers can access pictures you share online.
- Every single thing you write and every single photo you share on the Internet is preserved. It never, ever, ever, ever goes away. There are no take-backs.
- One time, in college, my roommate Googled her name and her cell phone number came up. That was back in 2006, when people still had home phones and landlines.

Just because she can operate a computer faster than you can doesn't mean she can keep herself out of trouble on one. The out-of-trouble skills are in a totally different category. This is a category where you have some expertise. If she's not kind on the Internet, she's not kind—and if she doesn't have common sense, prudence, and self-restraint in real life, she won't have it on the Internet either.

Technology Is Neutral

While Facebook has certainly upped the ante for the drama that teenage girls are capable of producing (and the trouble they're capable of getting into), I don't think that banning Facebook is the answer. Facebook is just the scapegoat.

As weary as I am of reading teenage Facebook statuses like, "Stop flirting with my man! You know who you are!" I am equally fed up with hearing parents gripe,

"Facebook is taking away her real-life friends."

"Facebook causes drama."

"Facebook is addictive."

"Twitter is making us narcissistic."

"Twitter is a time-suck."

"Pinterest is making us stupid."

"Pinterest is making us feel jealous and inferior as mothers and housekeepers."

I'm fed up with it because it's not true.
Facebook doesn't cause drama; people cause drama.
Facebook doesn't isolate you; you isolate you.
Twitter doesn't waste your time; you waste your time.

Twitter doesn't make anyone narcissistic; it gives people an outlet for displaying their previously existing narcissism.

I believe that social media (like almost every other thing) is neutral. It isn't innately awesome or innately terrible; it is what you make it.

I can say with a clear conscience that Facebook has never given me a single moment of anxiety. The teenagers I work with don't believe me because this sounds so otherworldly to them that it blows their little minds— but it's true.

The reason that Facebook has never caused a problem for me is that I refrain from posting anything that I wouldn't want every single person on my friends list to see. If there is one soul—one ex-boyfriend, one stranger—that I wouldn't want to know exactly how I'm feeling or what I did this afternoon, I don't share it publicly.

(Let me pause here to say that you and your daughter should both delete any ex-boyfriends and strangers from your friends list anyway. And stop posting things like, "We leave for vacation in two days!" unless you want your house to get robbed so you can bank the insurance money, which, for the record, is a terrible idea.)

Teenagers are shocked when Facebook doesn't treat deepest secrets (which they emotionally vomited into a public status as an outcry for validation) delicately. But the News Feeds of the masses aren't a diary or a trusted friend; they are the masses. Only a few people care; the rest are just curious. News Feeds are neutral, and if teenagers use them stupidly, the News Feeds will act stupidly in return. The degree to which teenagers overshare is the degree to which everyone else will butt in.

If you try to ban Facebook, Twitter, Tumblr, or whatever else, your teenager will resent you. She will say that you are overprotective and backwards. I don't say that to dissuade you, just to prepare you. If you have a strong conviction, or if your teenager's behavior has proved over and over that she cannot handle social media, then by all means, ban away—you're the grown-up.

But I think that a healthier, more long-term solution is to teach your teenager the principle of living with her filter on. It is with social media as it is with all of life: you have to take the good and leave the rest.

Take the enjoyment, leave the addiction.

Take the communication, leave the isolation.

Take the inspiration, leave the jealousy.

When I was a teenager, my mom taught me to read "with my filter on." She occasionally gave

> It is with social media as it is with all life: you have to take the good and leave the rest. #10things

me books, poems, and articles with bad theology, questionable morals, or colorful language. She'd always attach a note that said something like, "I loved this paragraph," or "Her metaphors are stunning," or "It's a very interesting point of view," and she'd close with, "Read it with your filter on."

What she meant was, "I don't agree with everything in here, and you don't have to, either." Take the good and leave the rest. Stretch yourself, think critically, learn what you can—and let everything else fall by the wayside. Art doesn't have to fit nicely into your worldview to be valuable; neither do thoughts or opinions. What great loss I would have experienced if my mother had sheltered me from everything with which she didn't agree entirely. My mom gave me boundaries; she taught me the things that she believes to be unequivocally true, and then she filled my world with art and music and books and news articles and told me to drink it all in—with my filter on.

Aristotle wrote, "It is the mark of an educated mind to be able to entertain a thought without accepting it."

Give your daughter a firm foundation, based on the Word of God. Raise her according to your deepest convictions and your best ideals. Give her structure and boundaries and truth—then teach her to approach this great big world with her filter on. Teach her to run the Internet through the filter of truth and wisdom.

You could ban Internet use, and that would probably quell the drama temporarily, but in so doing, you might miss the opportunity to equip your teenager with a principle that will shape and guide the rest of her life. What happens when she's out from under your roof? She certainly won't ban herself, I'll tell you that. If you've laid the groundwork and she is mature enough to have a filter; let her use it. Life isn't often all-or-nothing; she needs to learn how to take the good and leave the rest.

Test everything. Hold on to the good. (1 Thess. 5:21)

Three Questions

There are three questions that I use to determine whether or not a Facebook status (Twitter update, blog post, etc.) is worth posting. They aren't black and white; in fact, they're almost entirely subjective. No criteria, just questions. These three questions are my filter—my way to weed through my own thoughts and keep the best. I invite you to use them as a self-check and to share them with the teenage girl in your life.

1. What story am I telling?

The nature of social media is that, with our own words and pictures we get to write our own stories. People all over Facebook are telling the stories of their kids growing up, the places they go, the things they eat, the articles they read. The theme of your story is found in the common denominator of your posts. What do they have in common? What have you made your story about? Challenge your teenager to read through all of her statuses from the last three months and ask herself, "What do all of my statuses have in common? What kind of story am I telling?"

Is she telling a tragedy about all of her woes? (The weather is miserable, the homework load is impossible, her parents don't understand, her friends are fickle. All of these statuses usually end in ". . ." or "meh" or "siigghhhh.")

Is she telling a story about her emotions? (She's so happy! So in love! So angry. So betrayed. So sad. So overwhelmed. So confused.)

Is she telling a story about boys? (How much she loves her boyfriend, how much she wants a boyfriend, how that hot carhop at Sonic was checking her out.)

Young people today are living in a world in which most of their peers are telling the story of "WHAT I'M THINKING AND FEELING RIGHT NOW!!!" But Facebook is not a diary; it is a social media network.

A social media network shared by bosses, colleagues, exes, prospective dates, teachers, parents, grandparents, and friends. The things we write in our diaries are our thoughts; the things we share on our Facebook profiles are our stories.

Encourage the teenage girl in your life to ask this question before posting. Is what she's about to say worth contributing to the conversation? Will it help her to tell her story?

2. If I went back and read all of my Facebook statuses, would I recognize me?

It is true that our heat-of-the-moment selves are not our best selves. We think for a split-second, "I cannot believe how many people out there today don't use their turn signals!" But we aren't angry people; we just had an angry moment. Is your teenager's News Feed filled with her angry moments? Her lonely or gossipy moments?

Or is it a reflection of how beautiful she really is? Based on the things that your teenager has chosen to share with the Internet, would she recognize herself? Or would she think, *Wow, that girl sounds stressed.* In my experience,

> It is true that our heat-of-the-moment selves are not our best selves. #10things

57

most teenagers would be forced to say, "That's not the real me; that's not the best me."

Ask your teenage girl (very gently and seasoned with grace) if she were to read about herself, would she recognize herself? Even more, would she like herself? Choose to be her friend? Would she trust herself?

If not, why should anybody else?

3. If I went back and read all of my Facebook statuses, would I know that I was a Christian?

Jesus Christ is the most distinctive thing about me. My highest goal in life is to know Him and to make Him known, so if nobody who reads my Facebook wall could guess that I am a Christian, I'm not doing a very good job.

While the majority of what I write on my Facebook page is not explicitly about Jesus, I believe that everything there brings Him glory. I strive to live (and therefore post) in purity, humility, righteousness, love, and mercy. I endeavor to live and work in such a way that nothing I produce can malign the name of Christ.

If the teenager in your life were to tell her Facebook friends that she was a Christian, would they believe her?

When your teenage girl can answer each of these questions positively, she can be sure that she is contributing something beautiful to the global conversation.

Then Facebook, instead of a forum for passive-aggressive emotional rants, becomes what it is capable of being: a medium for connection, relationship, humor, encouragement, truth, and inspiration.

Chapter 4

Vegan Lions

*"It is not necessary to react
to everything you notice."*[1]

I have unfortunate Eustachian tubes. Does anyone know
what a Eustachian tube really is? I don't; all I know is
that whenever I get a cold, they fill up with fluid and my
ears punk out. My eardrums have ruptured a handful of
times and are now so damaged that every time a doctor
peeks in there he's all, "You know you're not supposed
to stick Q-tips in that far, right?" My doctor told me
that if my eardrums rupture again, I will start to lose my
hearing—at the ripe age of twenty-seven. This is terrible
information to give to a person who already jumps to the
worst possible conclusions, medically speaking, because
now, in my brain, the sniffles = certain deafness. And

that doesn't even sound crazy to me because the doctor told me so.

When I get the sniffles I go into DEFCON 1. I stop just short of pumping myself with intravenous fluids laced with echinacea. At the end of every day (during which I consume a vat of homemade organic chicken noodle soup and absolutely zero caffeine), my bedtime routine goes something like this:

Sudafed

Tylenol

Vitamin C

Zinc

Gargle with saltwater

(Piping) hot herbal tea with honey

Chug apple cider vinegar

Steam shower

Vicks VapoRub

Cough drops

Saline nose spray

Fresh air

Sleep forever

Everything except for a Neti Pot because, "Know thyself." I know myself, and I would drown myself. Or I would forget to sterilize the water and end up with amoebas in my brain, which makes deafness seem like not such a big deal.

While I was pregnant with Henry, I got sick. After a week and a half of my two-hour bedtime routine, my ears were still clogging up. It sounded like I was under-water, or on an airplane; the time had come to seek professional help. For as much good as the Sudafed was doing, I may as well have been popping Red Hots every four hours, which at least would have tasted better. Plus, after scanning my driver's license for the third time, my pharmacist probably suspected me of illegal activity.

I was sitting in the waiting room of the doctors' office when an elderly woman got out her cell phone and made a call. She called her law office. I know this because the volume on her large-screen, large-button, old-person phone was so loud that I could clearly hear the clerk on the other end of the line.

The only thing more awkward than listening to her renegotiate her will, discuss her real estate properties, and disclose all sorts of personal financial information (including the full legal names of her offspring) was what happened next.

As soon as the elderly lady hung up her phone, a second woman (who shall henceforth be referred to as "The Aggressor") whipped around in her chair and said, "There is not one single part of your brain that told you how completely inappropriate it was for you to have that conversation in here, huh!"

It immediately occurred to me that there was no good way for the elderly lady to respond. This wasn't a question, it was a statement. The Aggressor didn't speak out of concern or reprimand discreetly. She blasted an old woman and insulted her intelligence in front of a room full of people.

The elderly lady responded, "I'm sorry, I can't hear you, sweetie. I guess everyone in here is so stuffed up with colds, hee hee hee. What did you say now, sweetie?"

It was painfully sweet. Everybody in the waiting room shoved their noses deep into their magazines and pretended not to hear The Aggressor repeat herself and then threaten to go home and steal the elderly woman's identity—you know, to make a point.

Next, the elderly lady, still giggling, polled the waiting room. SHE POLLED THE WAITING ROOM.

"Was anyone else bothered by my phone call? Who else here was bothered by my conversation? Hee hee hee."

I thought, *Surely, surely, there is not a third person in this waiting room crazy enough to get involved.*

Alas, I underestimated the human compulsion to get all up in other people's business. A third woman piped up and said, "Well, this was neither the time nor place."

At which point I thought, *Forget it. I'm going home and going deaf.*

The point is, I sat there for fifteen minutes listening to three total strangers squabble and peck at each other in a doctor's office. As I watched this social microcosm unfolding, it occurred to me how much of the world's ugliness would be cured if we all just learned when to keep our mouths shut. Clearly, drama is not just a teenage problem.

————

Drama is a human problem. Drama is not something that teenagers deal with, but most outgrow, like acne. Drama is the fruit of ugly habits and bad manners, and there is no growing out; only growing up. When left unchecked, drama will follow a girl as long as she lives, like a shadow, like a consequence. Just ask anybody in the workforce, or anybody trying to get a date, or anybody who volunteers at church. The world is full of people acting like eighth-graders.

There is a direct correlation between how often a teenage girl says the word "drama" and how prevalent it is in her life.

"I am soooo not a dramatic person. I like hanging out with boys more than girls—girls are too dramatic. I hate drama so much. I am so sick of this drama! Will she just stop causing so much drama, it's like, it makes me so angry. Drama is stupid. Drama is ruining my life. I HATE DRAMA."

Huh. Methinks the lady doth protest too much.

To be fair, a teenage girl who insists that she hates drama might actually hate it. It doesn't take a rocket scientist (or even a GED) to see the mile-wide path of collateral damage. But since when has a little collateral damage ever interfered with a woman's guilty pleasure? Gossip, flirtation, overspending, overeating—hatred of a thing and participation in it are not always mutually exclusive. Your teenage girl probably does hate drama, but she also probably dives in headfirst and splashes around in the delicious, scandalous, emotional juiciness of it all.

> Hatred of a thing and participation in it are not always mutually exclusive. #10things

The drama deck is stacked against teenage girls. They are contending with sensationalist emotions, ruthless hormones, crushing insecurity, inevitable immaturity, and blossoming opinions—all set in a culture of oversharing. Throw a thousand of these creatures into a confined space that has a social hierarchy in play (oh, there are also a thousand boys and half of them are cute), and what can we expect except for these girls to go absolutely tribal on one another? It's a wonder more physical injury isn't inflicted in the halls of our nation's high schools. We have to nip this in the bud, y'all. Sure, I want our girls to live freer, healthier lives, but mostly I want to minimize the likelihood that they'll end up on *Judge Judy* in their adulthoods. This should be the highest ambition of every parent: to keep their children off of any and all daytime television.

While emotions and boys exacerbate the issue, the epicenter of drama will always be human longing.

Validation: Why I Watch *The Bachelor*

The reason that teenage girls are inclined to create drama is the same reason that I, a self-respecting adult with a college education, am inclined to watch *The Bachelor*. I hate *The Bachelor*. I hate the premise of the show, the gimmicks, the hokey rose ceremonies. I hate the prolonged suspense; I hate the mountains out of molehills and the anti-climactic cliffhangers. I hate what it implies about love and romance and marriage. I hate what the fact that I watch *The Bachelor* says about me as a person. Every year I resolve, "I will not watch *The Bachelor*!" And every year I pull up an episode while I'm eating lunch (or painting my nails, or while Dan is working late), and I cannot stop. My friend Cindy understands; she once said, "It has reached the point in the season where I'm embarrassed that I watch this show." It was the third episode.

The reason I can't stay away? I like to judge people.

There, I said it. Stop judging me about it!

Women judging other women is the driving force behind the success of this show. I am certain that the most-uttered phrases on Monday nights between 8:00 and 9:00 p.m. are:

> "That is not real love."
>
> "She's in it for the attention."
>
> "I saw that coming a mile away."
>
> "That is a codependent relationship waiting to happen."
>
> "They will never last."

And the number one most commonly uttered phrase must be:

> "That girl is insane," or the more colloquial, "That girl cray."

When women say these things, what we are really saying is, "I have insight! Look how right I am about this media-manufactured relationship!" It makes us feel wise, like we are more enlightened than all of those poor, beautiful women who have more hair extensions than they do common sense.

It is entertaining and validating, and it seduces us.

Teenage girls are seduced by drama in the same way, because validation goes down so, so smoothly.

If a teenage girl is longing to be heard, longing to be right—if she is longing to be smart enough or popular enough or liked enough—drama feels good.

It feels good to put her two cents in—to feel smart.

It feels good to offer her highly evolved opinion.

It feels good to gain allies—to cocoon herself with people who are loyal to her.

It feels good to pick sides—to stick up for somebody and to have someone stick up for her.

Drama garners a response, always, and it feels good to be responded to.

When I'm not giving my children enough attention, they do things like uproot all my plants and eat handfuls of potting soil because that's what it takes to get me talking to them, even if I'm talking angrily. Kids know when they can get more attention with bad behavior than they can by being mannerly. Likewise, teenage girls know, albeit subconsciously, that even though the response to drama might be gossip, outrage, or retaliation, negative attention is still attention.

"One who is full loathes honey, but to the hungry even what is bitter tastes sweet" (Prov. 27:7).

The drama fallout is certainly bitter, but if a girl is starving for validation, even drama can taste sweet.

Stimulation: A Poor Man's Passion

The second fundamental human longing at the source of Oscar-worthy drama is passion.

Women need adventure. Not just some of us, all of us. There is a wildness inside of every woman, a special kind of strength hiding in that second X chromosome. Loud or quiet, it's there.

My little girl is of the loud variety. She approaches every area of her little life with abandon; she laughs, cries, runs, and loves with the intensity of the fire of a thousand suns. I spend all of my time talking Madeline off of cliffs—explaining to her that things are neither as terrible nor as monumental as she perceives them to be. Madeline's favorite word is "ever." As in, "This is the tallest tower I've ever built! This is the best day I've ever had! This is the best ice cream I've ever tasted! This is the worst tummy-ache I've ever felt! This is the meanest Sam has ever been! He took my favorite toy I've ever had and threw it harder than he's ever thrown!" I have a newborn and a two-year-old and 80 percent of my parenting effort still goes to Madeline, bringing her back to center.

I have no doubt that she can change the world in the same way as Joan of Arc or Deborah the prophetess.

My best friend, Brooke, is of the quiet variety. She quietly started her own business, and it quietly became a smashing success. She quietly handles big tasks and undertakes big ventures. She quietly carries big hurts and forgives big wrongs. She quietly lavishes generosity, and she quietly inspires thousands.

I have no doubt that she can change the world in the same way as Mother Teresa or Emily Dickinson.

A part of even the most staunch homebodies (of whom I am The Queen) fantasizes about adventure like Sacagawea's—leading men through the wilderness, strong, capable, and brave—the heroine of her own story. Our souls need passion and purpose. When we can't find it authentically, we manufacture it in the form of drama and daydreams to feed our hungry hearts. The problem is that a woman subsisting off of drama and daydreams is like a lion subsisting off of grass, berries, and bugs. We might survive, but we will never be healthy, and we will never be satisfied.

Women crave adventure because we were created this way. God is on mission and, as His followers, so are we. He has a plan for you and He's got one for your teenager too. And the more I read through Scripture, the more likely it seems that it is not a safe plan.

Sarah left her life behind to follow her aging husband into some unknown "promised land" that she was just supposed to take on faith. She also ended up having a baby when she was nearly one hundred years old.

Rahab looked square into the eyes of the armed guards at her door and lied to them while harboring enemy spies.

Deborah led a battle. You guys, she led a battle.

Ruth knowingly settled in a hostile land and endured racial discrimination to preserve a relationship with her mother-in-law.

Esther went before the king on behalf of her people, knowing her beheading was likely. BEHEADING. Her cousin encouraged her, "Who knows but that you have come to royal position for such a time as this?" and Esther responded, "Go, gather together all the Jews . . . and fast for me. . . . I and my maids will fast as you do. When this is done, I will go to the king, even though it is against the law. And if I perish, I perish" (Esther 4:14–16).

That is a sense of purpose.

Life is a series of "for such a time as this" moments that are either seized, or not, and the girls that are out there seizing moments aren't involved in drama. Conversely, the girls that are entrenched in drama are never out there seizing moments. As I flip through the pages of my memory, looking back on all the teenage girls I've had the privilege to love, I am amazed at the universality of this principle. Girls that are training their backsides off for a spot on a traveling sports team, an athletic scholarship, or the Olympics aren't seduced by drama. Neither are girls that are organizing fund-raisers for cancer research or expending themselves to eradicate third world poverty. Career-minded teenagers that are job-shadowing executives and entrepreneurs don't have room for the emotional energy that drama requires.

Our souls know that the world, time, *life* is about something bigger than ourselves. When we feel disconnected from that, we try to amplify our lives to get just a taste of purpose. We are so hungry for it. We spin, stir, and fret; we busy ourselves and we talk, talk, talk to get a whiff, a drip, just a morsel of connectedness to the bigness of God that our hearts are after.

> *Our souls know that the world, time, life is about something bigger than ourselves. #10things*

We are mission people. Our hearts were created to be split wide open and to feel things. We were created to care about injustice in the world. We are on orders to care for widows, orphans, the poor, the hungry, and the persecuted. When those things begin to stir your teenager's heart, you'll see drama dissipate like a vapor.

Women crave purpose, but drama is easier.

Women crave passion, but drama is easier.

Women crave excitement, but drama comes much more naturally.

Drama is a poor man's passion, a cowardly man's creativity.

Drama is stimulation without any of the higher purpose—with no great calling, with no burden burning a hole in our hearts like a fire, with no risk, and no reward. Drama is an idle preoccupation; a cheap version of that which we really want, which is to live passionately on purpose.

———

A girl starving for validation and stimulation is danger enough; she is insecure and bored, a recipe for disaster. But what happens when these natural, universal human longings are compounded by bad social habits? Armageddon? You wish. As a parent, you will pray for fire and blood to rain from the sky, you will beg for earthquakes and floods and darkness and war and the end of all things if God will please just spare you one more dramatic encounter with that girl child. You will swear that if Jesus doesn't rend the heavens and come down, you'll save Him the trouble and send her to meet Him yourself.

Bad social habits are catalysts that shift drama into overdrive. And habits, when ignored, etch themselves into our personalities by repetition, like a river steadily carving itself into a canyon.

If you have the privileged authority to speak into the life of a teenage girl, part of loving her well is to take care to identify her habits, so pay attention. Encourage her to press into the ones that will shape her into a gracious human being, and labor with her to end the others, so that those relentless, repetitive waves don't carve her up any more than they already have.

The bad habits that fuel the most cataclysmic, catastrophic drama are things like oversharing, overreacting, defensiveness, venting, and retaliation. These reactionary habits are learned—and they are very often learned from Mom.

Baby Mama Drama

Women tend to be the primary managers of relationships in most families. They disproportionately care for children, aging parents, and keep in touch with friends. It is precious, rewarding work—to love people well, to invite them into your mess and to enter into theirs. It is also precarious work—peacemaking, discerning, communicating. Tending relationships must be done with consistency and grace; people must be handled with care. Your teenager is absorbing your social habits. Is she learning to handle people with care?

Maya Angelou wrote, "I've learned that you can tell a lot about a person by the way (s)he handles these three things: a rainy day, lost luggage, and tangled Christmas tree lights."[2] I would add slow Internet and getting stuck in a drive-through line when you are running late to this list.

When you are late and stuck in an excruciatingly slow drive-through line only to have your order butchered, what does the teenager in your passenger seat see?

If you vent, shred the service up one side and down the other, or blame the kids for moving like narcoleptic snails through cold molasses while you were hurrying out the door, your teen absorbs a sense of entitlement, blame-shifting, and verbal vomit, all of which, when applied to her own frustrations, lend themselves to hugely dramatic behavior.

But if your teenager sees you withhold judgment (perhaps the kitchen is short-staffed), extend the benefit of the doubt (perhaps the server is surviving a terrible day), and muscle through a frustrating situation, she absorbs a temperedness and grace that will stop drama in its tracks.

Once, when Dan and I were in full-time youth ministry, we had a family in our care that was so incredibly dysfunctional it defied statistics. It was as if lightning struck their family tree in twelve different places.

A beautiful, precious teenage girl hailed from this family, whose behavior was neither beautiful nor precious. She was simultaneously insecure and callous, which she handled by retaliating at everything with sarcasm. She interrupted, blame-shifted, and said things for shock value. She sought attention yet insisted on privacy. She pursued independence yet demanded coddling. She handed out ultimatums like they were candy and let friendships fall by the wayside when she didn't get her way. She overshared during prayer time, casually discussing all manner of private family problems: the ever-present threat of divorce, emotional abuse, and financial upheaval.

One afternoon we went to visit this girl at home, where we met her mother. Y'all—it was high school drama to the nth degree. The mother spoke about her daughter like she wasn't standing right beside her. She tried to validate her parenting to us by saying things like, "I've tried to tell her." It was as if, with every passive-aggressive jab, she was saying, "It's not my fault she turned out like this!" We felt so embarrassed for this young girl, who was being made to listen to a catalog of her faults aired out like dirty laundry.

As our relationship with this family continued, the mother would often call the church for help and be offended if it couldn't meet a given need. She volunteered private information under the guise of asking for prayer, and was indignant at any perceived inconsistency or hypocrisy in her fellow church members.

It became clear to me that this teenage girl's behavior was not the inevitable amount of sass gifted to all tweens on their twelfth birthday by the Teen Sass Fairy. It was a collection of learned behaviors passed down from parents who never learned how to rise above the chaos:

entitlement, insecurity, passive aggression, and a loose tongue.

At first glance, this family seemed to have been dealt an unfair hand—so many difficulties to overcome. But upon closer inspection, a large part of their trouble was a direct consequence of their drama. The universe wasn't out to get them; their habits were.

If the greatest culprits for drama are impulses—emotional reactions and immature thought processes—then the greatest weapons against drama are decisions—perspective, grace, and self-control.

Here is a one-minute primer on how to damper drama in your life and in your home. These are the practices you want your teenage girl to absorb.

Assume everyone is doing the best they can. Offer the benefit of the doubt. Mind your own business. Mind your manners. Choose your battles. Don't take it so personally; eliminate defensiveness. Evaluate. Am I speaking to help? Or am I speaking to feel better? Be humble. Be gracious. Don't believe everything you think. To the extent you control your temper and your tongue, you control your life. Wage war on jealousy; you are enough. Refuse bitterness—stiff-arm it. Don't react; respond. If you take pleasure in correcting someone, that is the time to hold your tongue; if it pains you, that is the time to speak in love. Don't let your mood affect your character.

Think bigger—pray for perspective. Practice empathy. Love people, love people, just love people.

The hopeful thing about habits is that, just as they can be learned, they can be unlearned. It's never too late. Years of snap judgments and emotional outbursts are no match for God's ability to transform. Do not underestimate the power of radical self-discipline and of grace.

> *The hopeful thing about habits is that, just as they can be learned, they can be unlearned. #10things*

Eliminate dramatic responses from your behavior and watch the teenage girls around you follow suit. Incredible. It's like they're watching us or something.

Let Them Eat Bagels

Whether the drama in your teenager's life is breaking your heart or making you want to tear your hair out by the roots, take heart; you have more influence over it than you know.

My mom was a Sunday school teacher once, for a fledgling little church full of friends. One morning, as she was preparing her lesson around the kitchen table, she looked to me and said, "Kate, I'm going to teach these little ones to pray. They are not too young to put their theology into practice. Enough fluff. I'm going to give them sustenance in the morning! Marie Antoinette said, 'Let them eat cake,' but I say, 'Let them eat bagels!'" Then she thrust her fist into the air like she was leading the metaphorical bagels into battle.

"Let them eat bagels" became an instant catchphrase in our home. Whenever we talked about something of real importance, something we knew way down deep in our knowers, the most sustaining, truest of things, we would say, "This is the real stuff of life; this is bagels!"

Your teenager is using drama to feed her hungry human heart. To quell the drama, put something better on her plate. Give her bagels.

If your teenager is starving for validation, feed her by listening. Real, eye contact, mm-hmming, listening. Tell her that what she thinks is important. Ask for her opinion. Don't finish any of her sentences even if you know exactly where they are going. Let her tell you, even when your brain is all "you've beaten around twelve million bushes, so would you please get to the point before I beat my head into this table!" Don't make up your mind about anything until you hear her out, and keep an ear out for how she feels, which is much more important than the information itself. Tell her that you're on her side. Tell her that she is beautiful. Tell her that you're proud of her for something—be specific and sincere.

Do this over family dinner, as you drive her around town, right when she gets home from school, or, if talking to you is right up there with kissing a slug in her book, talk to her while you take her shopping for a new outfit; she will not turn you down. *I* will not turn you down. I would tell you my deepest, darkest secrets for a new outfit; just walk me into Macy's and say "Dish." After all, parenting essentially boils down to eighteen years' worth of creative, age-appropriate bribes. Sorry, "incentives." Potato, po-tah-to.

If your teenager is starving for stimulation, feed her by challenging her. To occupy her is not enough. Aren't overcommitted busybodies (with enough stress and superiority to go around) some of the most dramatic people we know? Being on a cheerleading team won't keep a girl from drama, just ask, oh, anybody who's ever been to high school. But loving cheering enough to assume some extra responsibility, choreograph for a competition, to really pursue it, might. If idle hands are the devil's playthings, how much more are idle hearts! Busyness is not a drama deterrent; passion is.

When a girl opens her heart to the plight of orphans, the homeless, the hungry, the persecuted, the enslaved, or even the hurt and need in her peers, drama can't seduce her. The excitement of drama can't hold a candle to the excitement of a cause, a calling. When we stack drama up against the epic story of the real world, we see it for what it really is: petty, idle, divisive, and worthless.

Passion and adventure work like force fields against drama; idle words and worries get zapped and dropped to the ground by their extravagant hope and possibility. Maturity is not boring or lesser or tamer—it's greater. Do everything in your power to show your teenage girl

> The excitement of drama can't hold a candle to the excitement of a cause, a calling. #10things

what's real. Crack the door and let all of broken, beautiful humanity flood in like a sunbeam. Take her to a homeless shelter, take her to a marathon, take her overseas, take her to a neighborhood that scares you half to death, take her to a march to end modern-day slavery; she won't be able to unsee it. Let it in; let it move her. Let it inspire her, wreck her, challenge her. Let it change her. If you want her to catch the fire, you're going to have to put her near a flame.

As adults in Ann Taylor pantsuits and 8 to 5 jobs we sometimes get so bogged down with our small, immediate realities that we cop out of the greater reality. We tell ourselves, "I don't have the money to choose a greater reality; I don't have the zeal to choose a greater reality; I don't have the opportunity to choose a greater reality;

I don't have the vacation days to choose a greater reality." But all of those excuses are lies that you can stop believing any time you choose. We settle for gossip and Facebook News Feeds because they're occupying and engaging. But we're hungry. We are vegan lions in a constant state of craving, and at the first whiff of meat (or bagels) our breath will catch in our chests and we'll know: THIS, this is what I've been hungry for my whole life. Connection to the bigness, to God, to eternal things, to the mission. Ann Voskamp wrote, "It is us who want hard and holy things because we want more than hollow lives."[3] Yes.

God wasn't lying when He said that He owns the cattle on a thousand hills. He wasn't lying when He said that, with the Holy Spirit inhabiting us, we would do greater things than even the apostles in the early church were able to do. He was not lying when He said that He would be with us as we go to the uttermost parts of the earth. He was not lying when He said He would replace our heart of stone with a heart of flesh. He was not lying when He said that He was a consuming fire, that He would give us the nations as our inheritance, that He came to give us life to the fullest.

Do we not believe Him? Are we living in such a way that causes our teenagers to think that Jesus must have been speaking figuratively? That surely He didn't mean all of those things literally, because if He did, why don't

any of the Christians they know live like their God—
who is a consuming fire and owns the cattle on a thousand hills—has set them on a mission to save the world?
May it never be so. My daughter will find the smallness
easily, or the smallness will find her. May she learn about
the bigness from me.

May our girls learn about grace, self-control, forgiveness, kindness, and the great, big mission of God from
us. Among these things, drama has no place.

Chapter 5

A Pack of Wolves Is Natural

*"Sometimes I'm terrified of my heart;
of its constant hunger for whatever it wants.
The way it stops and starts."*
POE, SINGER/SONGWRITER[1]

*"That's where the truth lies, right down here
in the gut. Do you know you have more nerve
endings in your gut than you have in your head?
You can look it up. Now, I know some of you
are going to say, 'I did look it up, and that's not
true.' That's 'cause you looked it up in a book.
Next time, look it up in your gut. I did."*
STEPHEN COLBERT[2]

Follow your heart" is terrible, stupid, awful advice to give a teenage girl. The worst.

It is the worst because it does not translate. When you say "follow your heart," you probably mean one of the following:

"Do you know this is right?"

"Can you do this with a clear conscience?"

"Is this wise, long-term? Is this what you really want?"

"Do you really like him?"

"Is this something you truly care about?"

All of these are excellent questions. What'll ruin your day is that, in teenage girl speak, "Follow your heart" roughly translates to:

"If I want to do something, I should do it."

"Everything is a sign."

"If I don't feel like doing my homework, I'll follow my heart."

"If I want to take a nap, I'll follow my heart."

"If I want to make out with a boy in his car in my driveway before he drops me off for curfew, I'll follow my heart."

"Whatever I want is right for me, and if (inconceivably) I end up making a stupid mistake, it's okay because it was a crime of passion; I was following my heart."

"My heart will not lead me astray."

And all the women who ever dated a thirty-year-old man that lived with his parents or was addicted to Call of Duty or used too much Axe body spray or didn't know how to fold his own laundry or thought that Taco Bell was a legit option for Mexican food-date night will tell you—your heart can lead you astray.

You're going to have to start using better language before she follows her heart right into a cult or a pyramid scheme or a dead-end, codependent relationship because it felt right. Do you remember that warm, tingly feeling you used to get all over your body when you saw a boy you liked? That was common sense leaving your body. That itchy, eager feeling you get right before you let somebody have a piece of your mind is common sense evacuating your bloodstream. And that floating, invincible euphoria you feel when you're about to take a foolhardy risk, a gamble that is likely a colossal mistake, is common sense evaporating off of your skin.

Teenage girls subscribe to the ridiculous premise that if a thing is natural, it must be right. Come to think of it, it's not just teenage girls. The marketing departments of every food, cosmetic, and cleaning supply industry are engaged in a who's-more-natural-than-who battle that has escalated to cold war proportions. The last time I was in the grocery store I could practically hear the jars of peanut butter shouting across the aisle at each other:

"I have no preservatives!"

"Well, I have no high fructose corn syrup!"

"Well, I am made of peanuts and salt—no added ingredients!"

"Well, I am made with organic, locally grown peanuts, handpicked in the United States by celibate priests who washed their hands with sulfate-free castile soap and filtered water— and kosher sea salt."

The obsession with natural is fine when it comes to keeping chemicals out of your body and your home, but it's not a universal principle. Natural does not always mean safe, or smart, or right. As comedian Matt Kirshen says, "They say, 'It's safe; it came from the earth. It's natural.' Heroin is natural. Nicotine is natural. A pack of wolves, the edge of a cliff. What else? Look, I got you this big grumpy bear! Don't worry, he's organic!"[3]

This is my go-to cautionary word to teenage girls who are into following their natural heart-feelings. "Oh, you can't help yourself? It's chemistry, is it? It's natural? A PACK OF WOLVES IS NATURAL, SUZIE."

It's especially effective if you shout it with crazy eyes. Maybe spit a little.

The same faulty reasoning causes teenage girls to justify gossip and cruelty by saying, "Well, it's *true*." It puts me into orbit when teenage girls act like this kind of truth telling is their act of service to humanity. They say, "I'm just an honest person," or "I call it like I see it," or "I'm just saying what everyone else is thinking." Honey, the reason no one else is saying it is because they had enough decency to keep their mouths shut. I once told a girl in our youth group, "It may be true, but I'm sure there are a lot of things that are true about you that you wouldn't want me to tell all my friends." (I recommend erring on the side of grace, always, but a well-placed bit of sass can show a teenager that you're still awake.) That shut her up.

Just because a thing is true, doesn't mean it's necessary. Not all truths are kind or loving or anybody's business. Our standard for speech isn't truth; it's love. "Let no unwholesome talk come out of your mouths, but only what is helpful for building others up according to their needs, that it may benefit those who listen" (Eph. 4:29).

> Just because a thing is true, doesn't mean it's necessary. #10things

Our choices are subject to a similar set of standards. There is natural, and then there is right. Just because a thing is natural doesn't mean it's healthy or safe. The standard for our behavior isn't natural or intuitive; it's wisdom.

Jeremiah 17:9 says, "The heart is more deceitful than anything else, and incurable—who can understand it?" (HCSB).

Deceptive, incurable, incomprehensible. Yeah, what could go wrong?

The next time I hear someone tell a teenage girl to follow her heart I'm going to bust up into that conversation and be like, "Oh, you mean her wicked, deceptive, incurable, incomprehensible cardiovascular pump? The symbolic center of all her impulses and whims and selfishness? Nah, girl. You're good."

When you're talking to a teenage girl, you're going to have to be a little more specific. Tell her to follow her passions, her dreams, her skills, her opportunities, her brain, her intuition, her Savior—but for the love of humankind, not her heart. For her own sake, for the love of that sweet teenage girl, please, stop telling her to follow her heart.

Better Things to Follow

Passion

When you tell a teenage girl to follow her heart, she will pursue what she wants now. If you tell her to follow her passion, she'll pursue what she wants most. The difference will change her life. I enjoy thrift shopping. I enjoy puttering around my house, blogging, and keeping in touch with old friends. But when I sponsored a little six-year-old girl in Brazil, I told my husband, "This feels like the only worthwhile thing I've done this year."

I love leading small groups, building relationships, and teaching, but I cry when people tell me about selling their cars and homes and furniture and moving across the globe because Christ is worth it. Because His glory and the souls of men are worth it.

I have an opinion about immigration laws, foreign aid, marriage equality, and tax laws. But I openly wept when I read *Horton Hears a Who* as an adult, because "a person's a person, no matter how small."[4] The value of human life, no matter the level of ability or disability, moves me to tears. Foster parents make me cry. Adoption makes me cry. Special needs professionals and ministries make me cry in the best way.

We should pay careful attention to the things that make us cry.

We should pay careful attention to the things that make us cry.
#10things

In Greek, the word for "passion" is the same word used for "suffering," which I think is telling and beautiful. Louie Giglio once said, "Passion is the degree of difficulty you're willing to endure to get to the stuff that matters."[5] Exactly. How hard your teenager is willing to fight for something is a good indicator of how passionate she is about it. If she is willing to endure long hours, painstaking attention to detail, long practices, criticism from peers, or if she is willing to forfeit other opportunities, she might be passionate about something. About art, music, a sport, hobby, or cause—those are the things she should follow.

If you tell her to follow her heart, she'll pursue her hobby until it gets hard. She'll keep dancing or singing or playing until she gets bored with the technicalities and doesn't want to go to practice anymore. Her "heart" tells her it isn't worth it. That is one of the heart's great deceptions—telling us that things aren't worth it. If they are passions, of course they are. Our hearts seek the path of least resistance, and, unfortunately, we're all acquainted with the profound sense of loss we experience when we look back on wasted years. All the times we followed what we wanted "now" instead of what we wanted most.

Encourage teenage girls to follow their passions. Help them to see their own visions when their weary hearts have lost it. Help them to push through the hard and the monotonous to the place where it gets really, really good. Nothing good ever comes easy, and if girls are following their hearts, they'll never know passion because they'll never endure the suffering it takes to get there. Their hearts will take them into the shallows, full of splashing and play and frivolity. Passion will take them out past the breakers, into a deep ocean of awesome.

Dreams

There is an old Christian adage that says, "Bloom where you're planted." I guess that's fine in that we should serve Christ wherever we are, right this very minute. But when I hear it I can't help but think—*Who says I've been planted?* I am not a shrub, I am a person. I believe in doing the next right thing, and in doing what you can for who you can with what you have—so if that's what people mean by "bloom where you're planted," I guess I can get on board. But more often than not, I hear people passing down this little pearl when a girl is dreaming. When she wants to spend a year abroad, go on a mission trip to Indonesia, go to college in New York, or do anything new and scary. Dreams are birthed out of passions; they are full of hope and possibility. They represent our preferred futures, our ideals. They represent the best, most-awakened versions of ourselves—and they are worth pursuing. The most successful people on earth are dreamers. Big-dreaming is a skill that can be learned, and should be practiced. Leaders think big (then a little bigger, then a little bigger). It takes lots of guts to sustain big dreams because the constant risk of disappointment is so high. It takes discipline for a girl to set the bar high and work her tail off to reach it, believing all the while. Faith is not for the faint of heart.

The most fulfilled people out there are the ones who turned their dreams into realities—into careers and habits and lives. Please don't tell a teenage girl to follow her heart, and then, when she finally comes to you with something sincerely important to her, tell her to bloom where she's planted. No matter how audacious the dream, it's hers, and it's real, and you should never minimize it just because you're afraid of losing her. The dream may cost her a lot, but that's her cost to measure. Your job is to help her consider all the angles, to speak wisdom and encouragement. To plan, count costs, and pray. Don't scare her away from a dream because you are afraid. Her dreams might be enormous; they might be God-sized, and if they are also God-honoring, you can believe that He's in them. Be her prayer warrior, cheerleader, fundraiser, and her safe place to crash and burn. Remember that we need dreamers to challenge us. We need girls with vision and guts and discipline. We need girls full of optimism, determination, fire, and hope. We need big, out-of-the-box thinkers. Don't tell your teenage girl to follow her heart; it will only lead as far as her own self-interest. Her dreams, however, may change the world.

Skills

Your teenager is gifted. She may have been a stand-out in a particular area since she could walk, or perhaps she's still discovering and developing what will be her greatest skill set. She will have a spiritual gift and natural strengths and weaknesses that all intermingle to create a person-pattern that is only hers. I imagine personalities like equalizers—the little red and green bars of light that move up and down on the soundboards at recording studios. God is the great cosmic mixer, the brilliant engineer of personalities, dialing gifts, skills, and proclivities up and down.

> God is the great cosmic mixer, the brilliant engineer of personalities, dialing gifts, skills, and proclivities up and down. #10things

I have the spiritual gift of encouragement, but I'm also an introvert. I'm over-the-top organized, but sometimes messy, because I have zero self-discipline. None. I have a little bit of a teaching gift in that I like school, writing, and communicating, but research bores me, and I lack the insatiable curiosity that usually accompanies that gift. My optimism and enthusiasm is childlike and over-the-top, which is sweet but also maddening and irritating, especially if you're not in a great mood. I'm not the same as the other encouragers or the other teachers. I have interests and character traits that mix with my gifts and talents, and the output is Kate. It makes me perfectly suited for what I do.

Your teenage girl is perfectly suited for something too, and the opportunities she's offered will be a good indicator of what. What do people notice about her? What do people ask her to help with? What jobs, positions, and opportunities do people offer her because she came to mind? Instead of telling your teenage girl to follow her heart, encourage her to step through the doors that are opened to her. She is young, so don't fret about "Is this the best choice? Is this God's will for her life? What if she misses out on something else by doing this? What if she can't handle this or do it well?" What I know is that God is involved and concerned with the intimate details of our lives—of our days. I know that He guides and protects, and that a teenage girl (and those who love her) would have to blow through some serious roadblocks to keep walking down a path that wasn't healthy for her. This truth frees her to step through open doors, to walk into opportunities without the paralyzing fear of, "Is this the right thing to do?" If it's wrong, God will make it clear. He will make it clear through the Holy Spirit speaking to her soul, through her conscience and yours. He will make it clear through closed doors, obstacles, sound advice, and a lack of peace. If she veers off course, God will stop her short; He'll redirect. The

Good Shepherd always comes for us when we wander. So if there is an opportunity that appeals to your teenage girl's talents—her gifts, skills, or desires—encourage her to take it. Say yes; see where it takes her.

I was in the seventh grade when, to my astonishment, my parents said "yes" to a two-week exchange program to France. I was twelve years old when I brought home a flyer that had a picture of the palace of Versailles on it. Below was the time and date of an interest meeting and my parents said yes. I was afraid of not knowing the language and of staying alone with a host family, but my parents prepared and reassured me. That trip (which was based on my interests, skills, and opportunities) opened my eyes to the world outside of Raleigh, North Carolina. It opened me up to travel, independence, and a great love of languages, cultures, and people that are different than me. In hindsight, it shaped me in the best way. I love the things I learned there, and the things that trip forged in me.

In the face of God-ordained opportunities, a teenage girl's heart might feel scared. Her heart might be lazy or shortsighted, but her skills and opportunities will lead her well. If you both muster the courage to say "yes" together, you will be able to watch her life unfold in beautiful and unexpected ways. Keep taking the next step, and let the surprises teach her about all the ways God has gifted her and delights to give her good things.

Brain

Your teenage girl (most likely) has a brain. That brain works well; it's been keeping her alive for more than a decade. Her brain reminds her not to put her hands on stoves or jump into pools with her phone in her pocket. That brain has a decent track record, and it's high time she started listening to it when it gives her advice about stuff.

A good indicator that a teenage girl is not listening to her brain is how many of her sentences start with disclaimers. If she starts a sentence with, "No offense, but . . ." her brain is telling her "The thing you're about to say is offensive. Stop, stop, stop, stop, stop."

If she says, "I know you said such-and-such, but . . ." her brain is telling her, "You are about to get in trouble for not listening. You are disregarding or arguing with something you've been told. Give it up."

When we have to rationalize something, it's because our brains are telling us, "This is a bad idea." The worst, most hilarious, stupidest argument I've ever had with my brain was the summer before I left for college. Just out of a serious, heartbreaking relationship with my high school sweetheart, I'd been spending more and more time with a good friend of mine, as he was one of the only people still speaking to me after the breakup went down. One night, we were in his car, and I could tell he was going to kiss me. He was an honorable guy; he respected me, and we'd been good friends for a long time, so I wasn't in any danger, but I knew I didn't like him romantically. I knew I never wanted to date him. I knew that I didn't really want to kiss him, and I definitely didn't want to have all of the uncomfortable conversational fallout after the kiss. Those are all the things my brain told me. My brain said, "You do not like this boy. You are not attracted to this boy. You are leading this boy on. You are ruining your friendship with this great, great boy. Get out. Earth to Kate: YOU DO NOT EVEN LIKE THIS BOY!"

Then my heart retorted with the most idiotic argument ever. It said, "But you're seventeen. This is what seventeen-year-olds do. You have to kiss him so that you can make a mistake. What if you make it to eighteen without ever kissing a boy you shouldn't?"

When we have to rationalize something, it's because our brains are telling us, "This is a bad idea." #10things

And do you know what? I did it. I kissed him like an ever-loving idiot listening to her wicked, incurable, incomprehensible heart instead of her brain with the good track record. The fallout was awkward and awful. In fact, it was so awful that I only kissed two boys after that—and I married one of them. I still feel like an insensitive fool when I think about it. And don't give me any

99

slack. Don't say, "You were only seventeen." That's the reasoning that got me into trouble in the first place.

Implore your teenage girl to listen to her brain. Seventeen-year-olds can know better; I did. Logic, reason, and common sense—all of these are better things to follow than hearts. Hearts will tell them to kiss boys (that they don't even like) in cars late at night. I know all the mothers just had little bitty heart attacks because kissing boys in cars at night is literally the last thing they want for their daughters. I'm with you. Tell your girls to use their brains. Their brains have kept them out of trouble so far, which, I'm sure, is more than they can say about their hearts.

Intuition

Intuition is a real thing, straight up. Discernment is a spiritual gift. I believe in good vibes and bad vibes, and I believe they can save your life. Intuition is more subjective than logic or reason, but be careful not to dismiss it, especially if you are someone who sees the world in black and white instead of in shades of gray. Here is what your teenage girl needs to know about intuition:

If she is getting bad vibes from a guy, she needs to get out—fast. She does not need to spend even sixty seconds thinking about a polite or discreet way to get out, she just needs to get out.

If she is getting bad vibes about a job, she shouldn't take it. If an opportunity strikes her as shady, or a deal seems too good to be true, she should let it go.

If she gets bad vibes about a friend, she shouldn't confide in her. If she gets bad vibes about a church or a ministry, she should feel freedom to leave.

Intuition, I believe, is based on a collection of subconscious observations: body language, tone of voice, atmosphere. When there are coincidences, circumstances, or motives that we can't reconcile, something doesn't sit right. We can feel it. Dr. Joyce Brothers said it this way: "Trust your hunches. They're usually based on facts filed away just below the conscious level."[6] Women, as a group, tend to be more in tune with relational, social, and emotional subtleties than men are, so some of them have razor-sharp intuition, a real sixth sense. It is likely that your teenage girl is developing her sixth sense, so be sure to tell her to never, ever rationalize away a bad feeling that she just can't shake.

Intuition is also a helpful guide when it comes to speaking versus holding your tongue. If you want to say something, but your intuition tells you that maybe, just maybe, you shouldn't—don't. If you want to let someone have it, but your breath catches for just a second—stop. If you want to share something private, but you wonder for just a second if it's too much—wait. If you suspect that what you want to say might come across as bragging (or complaining, or critical, or hurtful)—stop. Share it another time and in another way.

Intuition doesn't just alert us to danger and trouble. Intuitive impulses can urge us into real acts of caring. It can prompt us to move toward other people when they, or we, need it most. For your teenage girl it might look like this: if she notices someone sitting alone at lunch and she feels an inner tugging—she should go sit with them. If someone is new to church or school or a team and she thinks, *I should invite her over*—she's right; she should. If she suspects that someone might need help or encouragement—she should be the one to do it, even if it seems out of the blue. Even if it doesn't make complete sense—just do it.

As an adult, if you know someone going through a divorce, or someone who's just been fired, suffered a loss, or is grieving in some way, and you want to say something, you should. You should say, "I love you," or "I'm sorry," or even "I don't know what to say." But don't ignore it because it's tender or uncomfortable. If you suspect that God wants you to reach out to someone, you do it. If you can't stop thinking about the homeless man on the corner, go give him some money. If you can't stop thinking about the elderly lady at the park, go strike up a conversation. We are relational beings, and (when adolescent hormones and pheromones aren't involved) our intuition is great at telling us if someone is in need of connection, or if they are bad news.

Intuition helps us choose between two good options, but not to choose between a good option and a bad one. If your teenage girl is stuck between two great jobs, she's free to use her intuition. If she gets to choose between two great colleges, by all means, she should go with her gut! If she's waffling between two stand-up guys that are both pursuing her, intuition is the way to go. But if one guy is sensitive and one is kind of a jerk, forget intuition and forget her heart, she needs to follow the voices of all the women who have gone before, because, we know, sweetie. We know.

The principle is the same for all of us: if one choice has a long list of cons, if everyone is cautioning against it, but something inside still wants to give it a shot—don't. When one choice is wise and the other is not, we don't need to think about it anymore. No praying or fasting required. If we are faced with a good choice versus a bad one, God begs us to choose the good. "I have set before you life and death, blessing and curse. Choose life . . ." (Deut. 30:19 HCSB).

Choose life. Choose health. Choose wisdom. Choose self-control. Listen to reason, to common sense and your brain. No intuition required.

God's Word

Sometimes I get frozen.

When twelve things need to happen at once and each one is dependent on the others—when there is no right order, no efficient course of action, I feel like I can't move my extremities. My brain locks up and I feel simultaneously overstimulated and paralyzed—hearing everything and affecting nothing.

It happens most often when it's 6:00 p.m., I have no dinner plan, the house is a disaster, all three kids are screaming, the baby needs to be nursed, Madeline has homework, and everyone needs to be in bed in ninety minutes. This happens at least twice a week.

My mantra when I get frozen and overwhelmed is this: "When you don't know what to do, do what you know to do."

It is my mantra when I feel aimless, like whatever mystical thing that holds my thoughts together, like skin, is gone, and I'm dissipating, drifting away from myself. When simple choices look like advanced calculus, I recite, "Just do what you know to do."

Deep breath, one foot in front of the other.

In my frozen 6:00 p.m.'s, what I know to do is to pick a child, any child, and hug it. I can't fix all the hurts, but I can fix one. Next, I clear one little corner of a room to function as a sanctuary. I throw armfuls of toys and laundry out of the way, wrap the babies in blankets, and sit them in the sanctuary with juice boxes. In clearing a space I clear my brain. My living room and my brain are connected in a mystical, spiritual way. When one is clean, so is the other—and vice versa. When I don't know what to do, I just do something—anything—that I know is right. I nurture something. Clean, fix, and solve something. Anything.

This principle—doing what you know to do—works on a grand scale as well as it does on a daily 6:00 p.m. scale.

The Bible, the Word of God, tells us what is right in every situation. It speaks to our actions, words, thoughts, and attitudes—it addresses our whole selves and how those selves interact with the world around us.

> The Bible, the Word of God, tells us what is right in every situation. It speaks to our actions, words, thoughts, and attitudes. #10things

When we are frozen or floating, we can pick something, anything, that God tells us is right and do it.

When you don't know what to do, it is better to follow Scripture than it is to follow your passions, your dreams, your skills, your brain, your intuition, or anything else. Scripture is the only safe choice.

There are so many decisions, so many crises, inherent in adolescence—it is one of the most defining periods in a girl's life. High school is filled with watershed moments, magic moments, where a simple "yes" or "no" will change a girl's world forever. So when your teenager comes to one of the million moments in which she doesn't know what to do, it is essential that she be grounded in the Word of God.

Prepare your girls for the frozen moments by teaching them scriptural truths that are always right, no matter what. Then tell them that when they don't know what to do, to just do what they know to do. Consider what the Bible tells us is right and good, and pick one.

Pray. Give to the poor. Forgive someone. Trust Jesus. Love God with your whole self. Get baptized. Love all people. Share your possessions. Tithe. Take care of other believers. Care for widows and orphans. Speak up for the oppressed. Submit to government. Use your gifts. Bear each other's burdens. Be thankful. Be joyful. Test everything, hold on to the good. Practice self-control. Resist temptation. Forgive again—and again, and again. Do justly. Love mercy. Walk humbly. Be gentle and respectful. Share the gospel.

Unlike her natural, deceptive, incurable, incomprehensible heart, these commands will never lead a girl astray.

Chapter 6

Get Mad, Not Mastered

"Emotions make good servants,
but bad masters."
ELLEN BOWERS[1]

My favorite commentary on female emotion is from the movie *Sleepless in Seattle.*

There is this great scene where Rita Wilson melts down into blubbery hysterics recounting the plot of the Cary Grant movie *An Affair to Remember.* She sniffles and chokes and fans her tears while the men in the room look at her like she has three heads. Then the men playfully break down into similar hysterics over *The Dirty Dozen.*

> **Sam Baldwin:** I just want somebody I can have a decent conversation with over dinner. Without it falling down into weepy tears over some movie!

Greg: She's, as you just saw, very emotional.

Sam Baldwin: Although I cried at the end of *The Dirty Dozen*.

Greg: Who didn't?

Sam Baldwin: Jim Brown was throwing these hand grenades down these airshafts. And Richard Jaeckel and Lee Marvin . . .

[*Begins to cry*]

Sam Baldwin: . . . were sitting on top of this armored personnel carrier, dressed up like Nazis . . .

Greg: [*Crying too*] Stop, stop!

Sam Baldwin: And Trini Lopez . . .

Greg: Yes, Trini Lopez!

Sam Baldwin: He busted his neck while they were parachuting down behind the Nazi lines . . .

Greg: Stop!

Sam Baldwin: [*Still crying*] And Richard Jaeckel—at the beginning he had on this shiny helmet . . .

Greg: [*Crying harder*] Please, no more. Oh! I loved that movie.[2]

The premise in this (masterfully-delivered) scene is the same premise that the world is operating on, universally: women are emotional. The scene is great because it holds up a mirror, and we are able to see ourselves in all our hilarious humanness.

According to the media (and dinner conversations amongst couples everywhere), we women are so emotional that our big, bleeding hearts can't help but dribble down all over the puppies we can't keep from rescuing onto the floor, past the overpriced school-fundraiser candy bars we couldn't say "no" to, and over to the television—where they soak our box sets of Lifetime and Hallmark DVDs. The presumption is that we have visceral, emotional reactions to breakups, weddings, and love songs, and that we literally lose control of our minds around babies. I can't object to any of this, as this year I've cried over commercials for the following:

> The Olympics
> Diet Coke
> Pampers diapers
> Publix grocery stores
> Hallmark cards
> Google Chrome
> St. Jude's Children's Hospital

Although I maintain that—male or female—if you've never cried over a St. Jude's commercial you are dead inside. I mean, come on.

While I cannot object to the fact that women are emotional, I have a major beef with the hyperbole—with the over-the-top jokes and jabs that pick at the "emotional woman" stereotype. It is fun—but it's dangerous.

The danger is in the nuance—the sneaky supposition that emotional reactions are unwarranted, out of place, or irrational. Hiding within every roll of the eyes, every humorous portrayal of a weepy woman, is the presumption that emotion is silly, weak, or lesser than stoicism. At the very best, any expression of emotion is simply misplaced.

I reject this presumption completely.

Do women often react to things more emotionally than men? Yes. But a reaction is not the same thing as an overreaction.

When women unquestioningly accept the "overly emotional" label, we subconsciously start to believe that our emotions are a liability and allow other people to treat us accordingly.

Here's what I see:

> Do women often react to things more emotionally than men? Yes. But a reaction is not the same thing as an overreaction. #10things

I see bosses, friends, coworkers, neighbors, husbands, pastors, and people all over every social media outlet dismissing the valid thoughts and valid opinions of women under the banner of "she's just being emotional."

I hear women apologizing for their feelings. "I'm sorry; I'm just a little emotional right now."

I see women expressing legitimate concerns that are too-often met with a patronizing pat on the back and a "There, there, it will all look better in the morning."

In other words, I see women getting dismissed and beat over the head with the "emotional card"—and I see women taking it.

Enough is enough. In order to protect our precious teenage girls from confusion, guilt, emotional abuse, and sexism, we must teach them to recognize the false presumption that emotion is a liability—to reject it—and to embrace the truth found in God's Word.

In other words, we have to teach them not to take it.

God Is Emotional

God created us—people—in His image. It's why some people are so endlessly creative and innovative, because God is the Creator, the Innovator. It's why some people are so brilliantly detail oriented, because they are reflections of a God who thought up organic chemistry and the quadratic equation and built an orderly universe.

It's why every single one of us needs community, because He (as Father, Son, and Holy Spirit) exists for eternity in community.

Our emotions are reflections of the very heart of God.

God loves.

God hates.

God gets angry.

God feels regret.

God feels compassion.

God feels pity.

God feels grief and sadness.

God feels joy.

God feels longing.

God feels hurt.

God feels jealous.

God feels satisfaction and pride.

God feels delight.[3]

God *feels*.

And our God Who Feels placed within each of us a soul capable of strong, furious, overwhelming emotion.

Not just women either. Men are emotional beings because they, too, are created in the image of God. Some men are more emotional than others, just like some women are more emotional than others. Logically, then, it follows that there are some men who are much more emotional than some women. They are not mythical unicorn men either; I actually know several.

As humans, we have the ability to be racked with sobs, to yearn and ache and howl inside. We can love so intensely that our chests leap and throb and ache. We can feel joy so deeply that the only sensation to which we can liken it is flying. The point is, we feel things, and our feelings move us—they affect us.

Our feelings are so instinctive that we sometimes get to be surprised by our own emotions. It's why we burst into spontaneous laughter, because we don't choose the joy as much as joy happens to us; it bubbles up from somewhere deep inside. It's why we gasp, squeal, sigh, and moan—because those noises are as immediate as the emotions that prompt them; we utter them before we have the chance to attach words to what is happening inside of us.

God knitted us this way, and I believe that it gives Him great pleasure. God doesn't shun human emotion; He doesn't tell us to suck it up or to get over it. No, God responds to human emotion. His heart is moved by our desperation. The prodigal's shame and humility caused the father to run to him (Luke 15:11–31). Hannah's emptiness and sorrow prompted God to give her a son

(1 Sam. 1). The bleeding woman's hopelessness and desperation moved Jesus to heal her (Matt. 9:20–22). The Israelites' contrition caused God to restore them—over and over again. Gideon's fear caused God to affirm and encourage him. God rewarded King David's joyous, flamboyant, get-your-groove-on worship of Him, and punished Michal for her snooty disapproval (2 Sam. 6:12–23). Throughout history God is not only emoting, but responding to His people's emotions with expressions of grace so divine that they could only come from a loving, feeling God.

> God responds to human emotion. His heart is moved by our desperation. #10things

God is emotional. Please, don't allow your teenager to see you apologizing for that which God placed inside of you as a reflection of His own divine character.

Think twice before chastising your teenager for her feelings, no matter how defensive, angsty, and ridiculously unfounded they are. No matter how "her own fault" her predicament is, no matter how preventable, immature, foolish, or shortsighted—there is still a person hurting under there; pray for the grace to treat her like a hurting person. Parent, you're going to have to pray for compassion. It's too easy to say, "I told you so," and "This is not the end of the world." But when you say those things to a hurting girl it feels like an attack, like you're kicking her while she's down. It feels like she's aching and hurting and all anyone can do is tell her how wrong she is for feeling the way she's feeling.

There is a time for setting straight, a time for learning lessons, but protect your relationship with your teenager first. Make your relationship with her one that she feels is worth preserving. You can do this by honoring her emotions. Correct the behavior, offer healthy perspective, but bear in mind: the emotion is not the enemy, the behavior is. Emotion is given to us—was given to your teenager—as a gift from The God Who Feels. Respect it as such.

Emotion Is Good

To say that emotion is good is so obvious, so undeniable and unavoidable; I don't know how anyone could argue. Without emotion we are shells of people, lower than animals; we are robots. Life and literature are bursting with stories about how—all terror, pain, and sadness considered—it is better to feel than not.

In John 10:10 Jesus says that He came to give us life more abundant—and abundant it is. The life of a follower of Christ is a roller coaster filled to the brim with high highs and low lows. God gives us huge burdens, entrusts to us huge hurts, and requires of us huge sacrifices. He also lavishes joy, peace, and love without measure. Life with Christ is full.

God gives us huge burdens, entrusts to us huge hurts, and requires of us huge sacrifices. #10things

Because we were created to live this full life, nothing less will do. This is one reason why men and women walk away from emotionless marriages. It's why emotionless friendships have short expiration dates. Our souls are meant to be intertwined with the souls of the people around us, tied together with love, trust, hurt, and forgiveness—doubled laughter and shared grief.

Because we have emotional souls created to live emotional lives, every single relationship—from spouses to fellow humans in the grocery store—benefits equally, though differently, from our ability to engage emotion.

Emotional Intelligence

With every passing year, leaders in the science, health, and business industries say louder and clearer that a person's ability to recognize and utilize emotions makes them more efficient, more likeable, and—bottom line—a cut above the rest. The "emotion in business" ball really got rolling in 1990 when two professors coined the term "emotional intelligence," and their research was launched into the pop-culture spotlight. In their influential article called, "Emotional Intelligence," Jack Mayer and Peter Salovey defined emotional intelligence as "the subset of social intelligence that involves the ability to monitor one's own and others' feelings and emotions, to discriminate among them and to use this information to guide one's thinking and actions."[4]

That's a fancy way to say that, when we engage our emotions, it makes us smarter. This flies in the face of the myth that emotion sits opposite of reason and is nothing but a liability in decision-making. The ability to recognize and process what we are feeling makes us less socially awkward, boosts our people skills, makes us better leaders, bosses, and coworkers, helps us identify problems, and helps us resolve conflict gracefully.

Studies continue to reveal the same thing: the best, most successful, healthiest leaders have high emotional intelligence. People with high emotional intelligence are more likely to get promoted, and less likely to feel stressed. It's funny, isn't it? When science and experience and common sense start to tell us what God has been saying all along? All truth is God's truth, and the importance of emotion is a glittering example of it.

Here are the four ways that emotional intelligence can work for your teenage girl, even now:

1. The ability to recognize her own emotions. *"I recognize that I am feeling defensive and edgy after the fight with my mom this morning."*

2. The ability to modify her own behavior according to the emotion she's experiencing. *"I am going to take a deep breath, shift my focus, and determine to have a positive, happy day at school."* Without the ability to recognize and respond to her emotion, a girl would spend the day tense and snappy, negatively impacting her schoolwork and her relationships with friends, teachers, and coaches, because she didn't have the wherewithal to intentionally shift her focus on the way to school. The fight and ensuing emotions would control her whole day.

3. The ability to recognize emotions in other people. *"I can tell by her tone and her body language that my teacher is tired and annoyed."*

4. The ability to respond to other people based on the emotions that they are experiencing. *"I am not going to ask my teacher for an extra credit opportunity today. I'll wait until she's in a better mood."*

A teenage girl's understanding of emotion benefits her enormously, even at a young age. When we teach our teenage girls to suppress, deny, or ignore their emotions, we take away an invaluable tool that God gave them to help navigate life. Emotion makes people smarter, not dumber.

Emotion Is Valid

In addition to teaching your teenage girl that emotion is good, smart, and of God, part of helping her to mature emotionally is to equip her with the liberating truth that emotion is valid.

I am absolutely over seeing rational reactions labeled "melodramatic" just because they are emotional. I am tired of hearing condescending statements like, "Chill out," "Don't get all emotional," and "You're not thinking straight" directed at frustrated women when frustration is the appropriate response.

Sometimes the right response is an emotional one.

Take grief, for example. Grief is one of the most profoundly necessary emotions; it must be acknowledged. There is no stiff-arming grief. It eats people alive when it's ignored; it steals souls. There is no way over, under, or around. Every one of us, at one point or another, will have to walk straight through it. Grief isn't logical; it's emotional, and as fallen humans living in a fallen world we are required to feel the full weight of hurt and loss. Grief is thick, tangible, and real. Grief is an emotion, and it is valid.

Anger can be valid. Jesus taught me that. Jesus shows us that anger can be righteous. The sex trafficking industry should make you angry. It should make you angry that the average age at which girls become victims of prostitution is twelve to fourteen years old. It should make you angry that roughly five thousand girls are trafficked and raped for profit every year in Atlanta alone. It should make you angry that babies are aborted just because they have Down syndrome; that should make your blood boil. The racism that Middle Eastern people, Hispanic people, and black people still endure in America should make you angry. Leymah Gbowee, Nobel Peace Prize winner, peace activist, and the President of Liberia, said it beautifully: "It's time for women to stop being politely angry."[5]

Hurt can be valid. Betrayal, broken trust, offense, conviction, and compassion all beget tears, and that's okay. When you (or your teenager) feel broken or moved, tears are good. When you feel compassion, tears are beautiful. You're not crying because you're hyper-emotional, you're crying because you're appropriately emotional. I love what Tina Fey wrote about being a boss and crying at work. In her book, *Bossypants*, she writes, "Some people say, 'Never let them see you cry.' I say, if you're so mad you could just cry, then cry. It terrifies everyone."[6]

And tears (lots and lots of tears) are a valid response to gratitude and grace. I will never forget one night in

July of 2007 for as long as I live. I was engaged to the man who would become my husband, and he'd just found out that I'd made a terrible judgment. It was an enormous breach of trust, a selfish, thoughtless action that cut my good, good fiancé to the quick. And do you know what he did? In the wake of the consequences of my own stupid decision, he stood up for me. He defended me, he forgave me, and he held me. In that moment, my fiancé was grace to me—and I wept.

> When you (or your teenager) feel broken or moved, tears are good. When you feel compassion, tears are beautiful. #10things

I wept with brokenness, gratitude, disbelief, love, humiliation, and relief. And believe me when I say, every single tear was warranted. As my very wise friend, Jamie, says, "There is not one single thing that is more life-changing than being on the receiving end of grace."

An emotional response to the gospel is a valid response. When you think about how your sins have grieved the heart of God, when you think about the cross and what it cost Him, when you think about the reality of hell, the preciousness of your salvation, or about the certainty of where you'd be without the pursuing, enduring, unconditional love of Christ—it should move you. You should feel something. If you can think about your Creator sustaining you, carrying you, and remaining faithful to His every promise without regard to your adulterous heart and not be moved emotionally, I submit that you've never really encountered God. There is no way for a person to understand the severity of their sin and the matchless love of God without responding emotionally. It's the only response that makes any sense. It should flatten you.

Emotion is valid, and my emotional, momma-bear heart cannot stand to watch the girls I love getting beat up and made to feel inferior because of their correct, healthy, normal feelings. If we want our girls to live in a society where women are heard and respected, we must equip them with the truth about emotion. The truth will set them free.

On Being Mastered

When you teach a teenage girl to honor her emotions, you free her from a lot of future guilt and shame, and lessen the likelihood that she will allow herself to be dismissed in the workplace or emotionally abused in a relationship. All very important. But if you don't also teach her not to be mastered by her emotions, you will create a monster. A sullen, pouty, entitled, mood-swinging, man-eating, fit-throwing, angst-filled, drives-her-mother-to-the-brink-of-insanity-and-back monster.

Newsflash: Emotions come naturally to teenage girls.

If you have been discussing this book with one such emotional teenage girl, chances are she's tracking with you on the emotion thing so far. "I have the right to be mad!" "It's okay to cry!" "God made me emotional!" "Emotions make me smart!" I've found that teenage girls are eager to embrace the notion that they no longer have to suppress or feel guilty about their plethora of emotions.

Learning not to act on every emotional impulse, however, is a much harder pill to swallow—especially considering all of the drama and "follow your heart" nonsense that they've been gobbling up like candy for the last five years.

In 1 Corinthians 6:12 Paul writes one of my favorite declarations in the entire Bible: "I will not be mastered by anything."

Part of living the Christian life is to be mastered, governed, by the Holy Spirit alone. Paul's declaration should be our declaration too. "I will not be mastered by anything." I will not be mastered by my selfishness, by my lust, by my hunger, by my alcoholism, by my substance abuse, by my anger, by my own impulses. I will not be mastered by pride or bitterness or unforgiveness. I will not be mastered by my hormones, my circumstances, or my thought-life. And I will not be mastered by my emotions.

My emotions do not control me; Christ controls me.

It is a crucial life skill for a teenage girl to be able to say:

> I will not retaliate just because I feel hurt. I will show grace because Christ controls me.
>
> I will not have sex just because I feel love. I will remain pure because Christ controls me.
>
> I will not scream at my parents just because I feel misunderstood. I will show respect because Christ controls me.
>
> I will not quit my job just because I feel tired. I will work hard because Christ controls me.

The ability to feel something and respond, instead of react, is the essence of maturity. My forever-favorite definition of maturity is this:

> Maturity is not a vague philosophical concept, but a trained ability to meet the demands of reality.[7]

I think that we, collectively as a society, should go all AWANAS on the teenagers in our midst and make them memorize that gem.[8] I think that I should be able to stop any given teenager on the street and demand that they recite the definition of maturity for me, on the spot. Who do I need to speak with to make this happen?

The degree of maturity in a person is the degree to which that person can meet the demands of reality, whether or not those demands seem fair. Meeting the demands of reality means doing things she doesn't feel like doing.

The inability to get emotions under control is what gives women everywhere a bad name. A woman who lets her emotions run amok is a fiery train wreck waiting to happen.

If your teenager doesn't learn how to get a handle on her emotions, people will stop trusting her. She will be the girl who cried wolf, who overreacted at every pass in order to garner attention or sympathy or admiration or praise. No one will be able to tell the difference between when she's really hurting and when she's just whining. She'll lose the support system she needs for when things get tough, because people will be hesitant to reach out and carry her.

> The inability to get emotions under control is what gives women everywhere a bad name. #10things

Her friends, boyfriends (future husband?) won't open up to her. They'll try to protect her from her own reactions; they'll keep things from her because they don't think she can handle it. She'll get too angry, too hurt, too sad, too overwhelmed. She'll miss out on meaningful relationships because her hyper-emotionalism will keep everyone at a distance.

Having and expressing emotions adds positively to every interaction (even professional ones). Being mastered by emotions torpedoes every interaction (even intimate ones).

A young girl mastered by her emotions is in just as much bondage as a young girl mastered by alcohol or cutting. It's a more socially acceptable vice, but if she doesn't learn how to get out, how to get control, the habits she forms will be detrimental to her adult life, negatively impacting her relationships, her career, and ultimately her own fulfillment and satisfaction.

Getting Control

In order for a teenage girl to gain control of her emotions, she must commit to continually check them against two things:

1. Truth
2. The Word of God

Emotions, while valid, must always be subject to truth. Just because a teenage girl feels something doesn't mean it's true. Can I get an amen? Just because she feels unwanted doesn't mean she is. Just because she feels right doesn't mean she is. Just because she feels her life is over, doesn't mean it is. Just because she feels like he's her future husband, doesn't mean he is. Just because she feels fat, unworthy, unlovable, insignificant doesn't mean she is.

Wrong emotions are still real; they are cruel that way. This is one of the most crippling things about depression: we see the senselessness of it—how arbitrary it seems—but that doesn't make it go away. We should always acknowledge a hurting person, because a hurt is a hurt is a hurt, no matter how it came to be. When this feels hard and torturous because, "For crying out loud, move on. Get over it! It was your own fault," I recite the Golden Rule in my head. It helps because when I'm hurting, even for ridiculous reasons, I want someone to see me. We need to see and acknowledge hurting girls, and a lot of times the best acknowledgement is, "I see you. I am so sorry that you are feeling this thing but take heart: It is not true, even though it feels true."

This is where a "it will all look better in the morning" can be healthy—when it isn't used to patronize or diminish, but to comfort. It doesn't matter how grown or tall or smart a girl gets, she will always need an understanding soul to stroke her hair and tell her everything will be okay. The feeling is real, but it isn't true; everything will be okay.

Not only do girls need to understand that their feelings do not equal truth, they need to understand that their feelings do not trump the truth.

> The Word of God stands unparalleled in its authority, which makes things nice and simple. Not easy, but simple. #10things

If whatever a teenage girl is feeling is in direct conflict with the Word of God, the feeling is wrong. Period. She does not need to pray about it anymore. The Word of God stands unparalleled in its authority, which makes things nice and simple. Not easy, but simple.

Freedom

Here is an activity I used when I was fighting, tooth and nail, to submit my emotions to the truth. It is an activity that the two of you could do together, that she could do with a friend, a small group, or by herself. Emotions are sometimes our biggest secrets, after all, and if you try to force vulnerability all you'll get is insincerity.

Have your teenager write down every emotional lie that she recognizes in herself, no matter how big or small. This isn't something she'll complete in an afternoon; this is something to start in a journal, a Word document, somewhere lasting that she will add to as she grows.

Down the side of her page it might say,

> I feel alone.
>
> I feel like nobody understands me.
>
> I feel like if anyone knew me, they wouldn't like me.
>
> I feel unwanted.
>
> I feel like the ugly duckling.
>
> I feel like I'll never be good enough for this teacher.
>
> I feel like I'll never be good enough for my parents.
>
> I feel like I hate her.
>
> I feel like I need him; if he dumps me I don't know what I'll do.
>
> I feel afraid of the future.
>
> I feel intimidated by the college application process.

And on and on—we have such a large capacity for emotion.

As she goes, challenge your teenager to match each feeling with a truth that directly addresses it. It doesn't have to be a Bible verse, though most of mine were, just something she knows to be real.[9]

After several months of recognizing feelings, recording them, and searching God's Word, your teenager will have a weapon. She will learn to wield the double-edged sword that the writer of Hebrews references: The Word of God, living and active, perpetually relevant. Eventually, her list might look something like this:

I feel alone. "Be content with what you have, because God has said, 'Never will I leave you; never will I forsake you'" (Heb. 13:5).

I feel like nobody understands me. "O LORD, you have searched me and you know me. You know when I sit and when I rise; you perceive my thoughts from afar. You discern my going out and my lying down; you are familiar with all my ways. Before a word is on my tongue you know it completely, O LORD" (Ps. 139:1–4).

I feel like if anyone knew me, they wouldn't like me. "For you created my inmost being; you knit me together in my mother's womb. I praise you because I am fearfully and wonderfully made; your works are wonderful, I know that full well" (Ps. 139:13–14). "But God demonstrates his own love for us in this: While we were still sinners, Christ died for us" (Rom. 5:8).

I feel unwanted. "He brought me out into a spacious place; he rescued me because he delighted in me" (2 Sam. 22:20). "The LORD your God is with you, he is mighty to save. He will take great delight in you, he will quiet you with his love, he will rejoice over you with singing" (Zeph. 3:17).

I feel like the ugly duckling. "The king is enthralled by your beauty; honor him, for he is your lord" (Ps. 45:11). "All beautiful you are, my darling; there is no flaw in you" (Song of Sol. 4:7). "Your beauty should not come from outward adornment, such as braided hair and the wearing of gold jewelry and fine clothes. Instead, it should be that of your inner self, the unfading beauty of a gentle and quiet spirit, which is of great worth in God's sight" (1 Pet. 3:3–4).

I feel like I'll never be good enough for this teacher. I feel like I'll never be good enough for my parents. "But he said to me, 'My grace is sufficient for you, for my power is made perfect in weakness.' Therefore I will boast all the more gladly about my weaknesses, so that Christ's power may rest on me" (2 Cor. 12:9). "Am I now trying to win the approval of men, or of God? Or am I trying to please men? If I were still trying to please men, I would not be a servant of Christ" (Gal. 1:10). "Whatever you do, work at it with all your heart, as working for the Lord, not for men" (Col. 3:23).

I feel like I hate her. "For our struggle is not against flesh and blood, but against the rulers, against the authorities, against the powers of this dark world and against the spiritual forces of evil in the heavenly realms" (Eph. 6:12). "You have heard that it was said, 'Love your neighbor and hate your enemy.' But I tell you: Love your enemies and pray for those who persecute you" (Matt. 5:43–44).

I feel like I need him; if he dumps me I don't know what I'll do. "I am he, I am he who will sustain you. I have made you and I will carry you; I will sustain you and I will rescue you" (Isa. 46:4). "The LORD appeared to us in the past, saying: 'I have loved you with an everlasting love; I have drawn you with loving-kindness'" (Jer. 31:3).

I feel afraid of the future. "'For I know the plans I have for you,' declares the LORD, 'plans to prosper you and not to harm you, plans to give you hope and a future'" (Jer. 29:11).

I feel intimidated by the college application process. "For God did not give us a spirit of timidity, but a spirit of power, of love and of self-discipline" (2 Tim. 1:7). "I can do everything through him, who gives me strength" (Phil. 4:13).

Imagine how your teenager's life would be revolutionized if she were able to combat her emotions with that list of empowering truths!

My personal list has been a treasure to me. My list has given me wits when I had no wits about me. The Word of God centers us, focuses us, and tells us the truth—it will tell your teenage girl the truth. When her emotions are threatening to leech the sense and logic right out of her, when they feel oppressive and suffocating and like the only real thing in the world, the Word of God is a lifeline back to reality. A list like this gives her the ability to feel what she's feeling (to write it down, to validate it) and then to submit those very real feelings to the very real truth.

When we teach our teenage girls to view emotion correctly, we give them the freedom to embrace their emotions, the ability

> The Word of God centers us, focuses us, and tells us the truth—it will tell your teenage girl the truth. #10things

to experience the magic of them fully, and the power to subject their emotions to the truth. In so doing, we usher our girls toward greater confidence and maturity. This is the essence of leadership—of parenting. There is so much hope for the world; young women freed from the bondage of insecurity and grounded in truth and power of God are a force to be reckoned with.

Chapter 7

Smoking Is Not Cool

"One in three youth smokers will eventually die from a tobacco-related disease."[1]

Smoking is not cool.

Chapter 8

Six Circles

"Let us live so that when we come to die
even the undertaker will be sorry."
MARK TWAIN[1]

"Regard your good name as the richest jewel you
can possibly be possessed of—for credit is like fire;
when once you have kindled it you may easily
preserve it, but if you once extinguish it, you will
find it an arduous task to rekindle it again.
The way to a good reputation is to endeavor to
be what you desire to appear."
SOCRATES[2]

A teenage girl who insists she doesn't care what anybody thinks about her is like a heroin addict who insists she can "quit any time she wants." That which they claim not to need is the very thing that consumes them. There is no more trend-conscious, fashion-conscious, reputation-conscious, approval-seeking creature on the planet than a teenage girl. That's not a jab; it is a reality. There are entire industries that exist solely because teenage girls care what other people think. There is a litany of medical and psychological disorders that spring from a teenage girl's obsession with what other people think. Thousands of grown women are in therapy every day because they cared what their fathers thought of them—what their mothers, friends, and classmates thought.

Eighty percent of the decisions a girl makes in a day are made with the aim to be well-liked: hair, clothes, music, weekend plans, the jobs she applies for, the language she uses, and the company she keeps—for starters.

Sometimes girls assume that because they have no desire to infiltrate the "in crowd," that they don't care what people think about them—popularity isn't their aim. But caring what people think isn't about popularity; it's about belonging. Girls who hate cheerleaders usually go to great lengths to differentiate themselves from cheerleaders, effectively proving that they do care about how they are perceived—they just want to be perceived as different. Caring about what people think isn't just for the insecure and the wannabes. The desire to belong to any group or non-group—the desire to be associated or disassociated from anyone or anything—is to care what people think.

What's more, to teenage girls, independence, free-thinking, and a little rebellion are cool—in every social circle, no matter how mainstream or how obscure. If a girl gets a reputation for caring what other people think, she's called desperate, insecure, shallow, or a mindless sheep. There is no scarlet letter in girl-dom as shameful as caring what people think. (Except for maybe dating a friend's ex.) It is very important to girls that they be perceived as the type of people who don't care what other people think. The irony.

Humans are natural image-guarders, and teenage girls take image guarding to a whole 'nother level. The list of things a teenage girl will compromise, or downright sacrifice, to feel like she belongs is long and terrifying.

When a teenage girl says, "I don't care what you think about me," it's never true. What she means is, "I don't care what this particular person thinks," or "I don't care what you think about this issue" (her clothes, her boyfriend, whatever), or "You don't have all the facts about me, so your opinion is incorrect and irrelevant."

But she cares what people think about her—about who she is and what she's worth. I know because we all do. Belonging is one of the most powerful motivators.

It isn't just teenagers, and it isn't just girls. All of us would run the gamut of *Fear Factor*'s worst—without blinking—if we knew that, at the end, was belonging.

We would think, "So you're telling me that there will be a community of people that enjoy each other and carry each other along? There will be no loneliness or insecurity? I will be appreciated, needed, and missed when I'm not there? I'll be understood, truly known, and loved? I can be a part of something bigger than myself? I'll have a home, a niche? Okay. I'll walk across fire for that. I'll climb into that bathtub full of leeches—as long as there is a tribe of friends to pull me out on the other side, and care for me."

Caring what other people think is not born of weakness or insecurity. It is born of the need for relationship—and it is a need. God saw that it wasn't good for man to be alone, and our primal desires for love, affirmation, validation, and friendship are reflections of that truth. Those impulses are tells—soul cravings. Community is how we were created to live. Community is the way we experience the love of God, through His people. Caring what people think is not a character flaw. The degree to which teenage girls care what people think doesn't make them egocentric or even insecure; it makes them human. They are nothing but grown-up versions of

> Caring what other people think is not born of weakness or insecurity. It is born of the need for relationship.
> #10things

toddlers in Cinderella dresses; they still need a safe place to land. They are nothing but baby versions of wives and mothers; they already need a support system.

Please don't make teenage girls feel like imposters because they care about what people think of them. Stop telling them not to care. Caring what other people think is not the form of mental slavery we make it out to be; it's not insincere, shallow, or selling out. There is middle ground between obsession with popularity and total disregard for one's reputation. Girls don't automatically lose sight of their true selves just because they care.

There is no need to wear "I don't care" like a badge of honor—not for them and not for you. Not caring doesn't make you stronger than anybody else. Usually, it just makes you lonelier.

Percentages

I am terrible at higher math. Really, really atrocious. I hung with math through Algebra 1, and I was actually kind of awesome at Geometry, but after Geometry comes Algebra 2, and that's where it went downhill. I failed my very first test in my entire academic career when I had to graph parabolas (or paraboles, or hyperboles, or hyperbolas or whatever they are called). When I did, something inside my Type A, first-born, irrationally competitive, eager-to-please heart broke, and math was dead to me. It does not matter how many math majors try to explain it, I still maintain that there is absolutely no point in having imaginary numbers. If I'm going to be imagining things, I'd much rather imagine fanciful worlds from *Where the Wild Things Are* than a bunch of make-believe numbers. Lame.

One of the subjects in math that I'm especially bad at is percentages. Every time I see a problem having to do with ratios or interest rates, something in my brain short-circuits. There is a pop, fizzle, and a puff of smoke and everything from that point forward is 100 percent made up (made-up answers are a kind of imaginary number I can get on board with). This makes me a great tipper at restaurants; one time my husband looked over my shoulder and said, "Kate, you're leaving a 40 percent tip." Whoops.

I'd like to give teenage girls the benefit of the doubt here. Maybe the reason they are so hot or cold about what people think about them—obsessing over it or rejecting it altogether—is not because they are immature or in denial, maybe they are just bad at math, like me. Maybe the notion that some people's opinions should carry more weight than others is entirely too much percentage-math to bother with.

Teenage girls need a brave soul to delve into this messy gray area with them and to show them that everything doesn't count 100 percent. All opinions are not equal.

When we equip girls to choose whose opinions to listen to and when, we set them free. We tell them, "You are allowed to care, allowed to need friends, and allowed to value a good name. You are allowed to listen to what's true, but you're also allowed to ignore what isn't. You get to choose which voices stick and which voices fall by the wayside."

———

In the life of every teenage girl there are some recurring characters: God, herself, her parents, her friends, classmates, and strangers. The opinions of every single one of these recurring characters matters—they just don't matter the same.

Here is a simple breakdown:

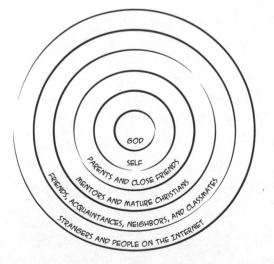

God

Bottom line: God is the only One operating with all of the information. When people form opinions about your teenage girl, they do so by collecting clues from her appearance, her personality, her choices, the company she keeps, and whatever other measure of popularity and worth that seems so important at the time.

Only God knows every minute of every day she ever lived. (Heb. 4:13)

Only God knows her innermost thoughts. (Ps. 139:1–4)

Only God knows every hurt, every motivation, every experience, big or small, that has shaped her in any way.

Only God is working with all the information. (Rom. 2:2)

In the Old Testament, God is called *El Roi*, "God who sees." Is that not the most glorious thing you've ever heard? God who sees. He sees me. He sees you. He sees us. And He sees your teenage girl. At the end of her life, when your teenage girl stands before God, she stands before the only One who has ever really known her.

Nobody else has the authority to say where your teenager will spend eternity or why. No person, no matter how much they know, how loudly they speak, or how many people they influence, can add or detract a speck of value from your teenage girl's life—thank God. It is your duty to make this clear to her. God has spoken, and He says she is the apple of His eye—end of discussion. On days that you could wring her neck, she's enough. On days she's made colossal mistakes, she's enough.

> When a young woman sets out to determine her worth—when she considers how much she is loved and how deeply—God's Word is final. #10things

When a young woman sets out to determine her worth—when she considers how much she is loved and how deeply—God's Word is final. If He says she needs to be saved, she does. If He says she's sin-sick, she is. If He says she is forgiven, she is. If He says she's pure and lovely, she is.

In this supreme sense, God's opinion of her is the only one that matters.

Self

Second only to God, your teenage girl knows more about herself than anybody else does.

In your young life, there were delicate dreams, secret desires, and injuries of heart that your parents knew not of. The same is true of your teenage girl, no matter how open and amicable your relationship. She has a lifetime's worth of thoughts and feelings that she hasn't shared with you. Some she may have willfully hidden, but, mostly, she can't communicate the sheer volume of them; no one can. Her life is littered with conversations, experiences, relationships, and lessons that will only ever be hers, privately. Such is personhood—so much happens to us when we are alive.

You may be able to sense your teenager's mood swings coming like an old man's trick hip can sense the rain. You may be able to spot tendencies and patterns in her life before she recognizes them for herself, but bear in mind that you are wise—not omniscient. I love Rose's line from the movie *Titanic*, "A woman's heart is a deep ocean of secrets." What starts as a puddle of private feelings in childhood grows into an ocean by adolescence.

When we value the opinions of other people over what we know to be true, those false labels wrap themselves around our hearts like hungry boa constrictors. They squeeze—gently, steadily—until they strangle our hearts to death. Death by insecurity and frantic people-pleasing.

Give your daughter permission to believe the truth about herself. God's truth, and then her own—even when they are the only two who know it.

Parents

Moms, go ahead and climb up on your soapboxes; this one's for you. You're welcome. The opinions of parents carry more weight than the opinions of anyone in the outer rings of the circle for two reasons.

1. They know their kids.
2. Teenagers are under orders to honor them.

Bam.

Parents (or whichever family members a teenager grows up with) have observed, almost scientifically, their children from the moment of their births. They watched their teenager's personality come to life long before she could even talk. They know whether each child is strong-willed or easy-going, what things motivate and scare them. They've spent years listening. Apart from God and herself, the people who know a teenage girl best are her parents.

Teenagers will contest this. They believe that their friends know more about them because they tell their friends more than they tell their parents. Friends may have more information, but parents have more insight.

Friends might know more, parents know deeper. Parents possess a breed of wisdom that only comes by experience—they earned it with age. A dad might not know who his daughter has a crush on this week, but he could pick her out of a crowded football stadium in two hot seconds by her gait.

Children are commanded to honor these parents that know them. This commandment does not expire when a child turns eighteen. When a girl is young, honor means obey. When she becomes independent, honor does not necessarily mean obey, though it can. It does mean listen. It means respect, love, serve, and consider greater than yourself. As a grown woman, I can do things that my parents don't love, but to remain in good conscience (and right with God), I must honor them.

Moms, you birthed that girl, and it was gory. You fed her, and she bit you. You cleaned her own filth off of her for nearly a decade. You survived the terrible twos and only exposed her to a small bit of profanity when you couldn't strap the car seat into the car. You comforted more tantrums than you videotaped, and that earns you the right to speak to your teenage girl's actions and thoughts in a unique way. She must do more than just consider your opinion, she must value it.

Note: I include mature Christians in this category too. They have the same wisdom born of age, and as brothers and sisters in Christ, they have the Word of

God and the Holy Spirit as their guide. If a pastor or mentor shares an opinion in love, Sally-SassyPants should listen up.

Best Friends

The opinions of friends matter for one big, gigantic reason: relationships matter.

Eventually, your daughter's best friend will misunderstand her—maybe even betray her. One day your daughter will be offended by her best friend. A teenage girl offended by something? Shocking, I know.

Her friends will tell her that they hate her boyfriend, they just will. They may tell her that the college she chose is a waste of her time. They may tell her that she's being dumb, shallow, mean, selfish, jealous, dramatic, or any number of other things that teenage girls are to each other. Maybe they'll be right and maybe they won't, but their rightness is largely irrelevant.

> The opinions of friends matter for one big, gigantic reason: relationships matter.
> #10things

Friends don't get to dismiss the opinions of friends out of hand just because they disagree. That kind of close-minded defensiveness is a quick way to kill friendships.

There is an enormous difference between caring what friends think and internalizing everything they say, and making choices to appease people. No one should live their lives at the mercy of the fickle, uninformed opinions of other people; that's insane. But neither can we disregard them; that's unwise (see Gal. 1:10).

When girls grow up, they need someone who knows them—someone who knows all their stories. When she is twenty-five years old, your daughter will need someone she can call at eleven o'clock at night because she's having the worst day. She will need someone who is committed enough to their friendship to buy a plane ticket to come and visit—someone that hasn't just heard about her struggles, but has walked through them with her. She will need someone who has loved her at her ugliest, forgiven her, and stuck around. We all need someone we can trust completely.

One of the most beautiful descriptions of a friend was written by Dinah Maria Craik when she said,

> Oh, the comfort, the inexpressible comfort of feeling safe with a person; having neither to weigh thoughts nor measure words, but to pour them all out, just as they are, chaff and grain together, knowing that a faithful hand will take and sift them, keep what is worth keeping, and then, with the breath of kindness, blow the rest away.[3]

It takes years, tears, and compromise to build a friendship like this. It doesn't happen overnight, no matter how much a pair has in common. If you encourage your teen to disregard every hurtful opinion, you will make it near-impossible for her to build a friendship like this. You will cripple her.

Girls must learn to care about things they wouldn't ordinarily care about for the sake of another person. This is the essence of selflessness. It is evidence of maturity and necessary for friendship.

While the opinions of friends don't determine your daughter's value (only God can do that), and they don't carry the same weight as absolute truth, they matter.

They matter because friends matter.

Community

A girl's community is comprised of all the people she sees on a regular basis: her classmates, teammates, neighbors, boys she has a crush on, people she babysits for, and Starbucks baristas. The impression that this eclectic group of people holds of her is known as her "reputation."

Reputation, in the language of teenagers, is synonymous with stereotype, rumor, and unfounded prejudgment. On this point teenagers need to be set straight. Reputation does not mean, "stuff people make up, imagine, or presume about you." Reputation means, "the things you are known for."

If the consensus in a teenage girl's community is that she is a snob, it means that this great, varied assortment of people (Republicans, Democrats, old, young, Christians, atheists, and everyone in between) who disagree on virtually every other thing collectively agree that she is a snob.

This is a major red flag.

One person can misjudge a girl; a group of friends can misjudge a girl. But if a girl is known by her community as a snob? It either means that she is, or that whatever she's putting out there is making her appear to be.

It's like eyewitnesses in a court case. If one person claims to have seen something, there's a chance they are mistaken. If ten people saw it, it's probably true. But if two hundred strangers standing on a crowded street all describe the exact same incident in perfect detail? Bang the gavel, case closed—book 'em.

Our communities are on the witness stand, our behavior is the evidence, and the verdict is our reputation.

If your teenager has a reputation for being snide (or a flake, or of not keeping her word), it matters. A bad reputation is an indictment on her character. It should matter to her if every person she comes into contact with walks away from the interaction thinking she's snide. Either everyone is right—in which case she should make some major changes to her character—or everyone is wrong—in which case she should make some major changes to her behavior. Either way, she's got a problem on her hands.

Our communities are on the witness stand, our behavior is the evidence, and the verdict is our reputation. #10things

The opinions of others cannot detract value from anybody's life, but they can detract credibility, and credibility matters.

Reputation matters because:

1. She wants friends to like her and trust her.
2. She wants teachers to give her a break when she forgets her homework.
3. She'll have to meet her boyfriend's parents someday.
4. She's going to need a job someday.
5. One day she's going to need help moving furniture and nobody is going to volunteer their truck if they think she's a snob.

Don't inadvertently teach your teenage girl to ignore her reputation in the name of empowering her. She can be perfectly self-assured and still be aware of the impression she leaves on those around her.

"A good name is more desirable than great riches; to be esteemed is better than silver or gold" (Prov. 22:1). When

> We should all endeavor to live so that, if anyone were to speak ill of us, no one would believe them. #10things

a young lady lives with integrity and grace, a good reputation will inevitably follow. If anyone speaks ill of her, her community will come to her defense: "Oh, you must have caught her on a bad day. Perhaps there was a misunderstanding. That is not the girl we know." We should all endeavor to live so that, if anyone were to speak ill of us, no one would believe them.

Strangers on the Internet

The opinions of strangers on the Internet carry the least weight of all. They know little to nothing about us, and what they do know is only what we choose to share. Presumptions from such people are shallow at best, and often baseless. Teenage girls mustn't live by the praise of strangers on the Internet—hits on a blog, likes on an image. It's a trap.

Here's what I learned when I started a blog: a lot of people don't like me—and most of them are on the Internet. No teenage girl can police the Internet from her bedroom. She can't answer every objection or address every criticism. Internet critics are like gray hairs;

you pick one off and three more show up in its place. A teenage girl would have an easier time wrangling a pig greased with butter than she would trying to explain and defend herself to Internet trollers; it's an uphill battle—and it's up the wrong hill. A girl must know that those ill-informed, critical words are not worth the energy it takes to dwell on them for one more minute. We can't make everyone like us; I hate that. Your teenage girl can't make everyone like her. What she can do is behave in a way that reflects her nature, a way that is becoming to a follower of Jesus.

While strangers don't have much authority to speak to the issues in your teenager's life, the way she presents herself to them still matters. It matters because God says it does.

> "By this all men will know that you are my disciples, if you love one another." (John 13:35)

> "In the same way, let your light shine before men, that they may see your good deeds and praise your Father in heaven." (Matt. 5:16)

> Do this with gentleness and respect, keeping a clear conscience, so that those who speak maliciously against your good behavior in Christ may be ashamed of their slander. (1 Pet. 3:15–16)

"A good tree cannot bear bad fruit, and a bad tree cannot bear good fruit. . . . Thus by their fruit you will recognize them." (Matt. 7:18, 20)

The fruit of the Spirit is love, joy, peace, patience, kindness, goodness, faithfulness, gentleness and self-control. (Gal. 5:22–23)

These biblical mandates don't jibe with "I don't care what anybody else thinks of me."

As Christians, our job is to point others—everyone, strangers—to Christ. We are to be known as loving people, givers and forgivers. We should be noticeably full of joy, patience, kindness, gentleness, and self-control—proof that the Holy Spirit is real and living and governing our lives.

Our society is guilty of selling teenagers half-truths wrapped up as encouragement and pithy advice. "It doesn't matter what other people think about you," is not true. It's half true. And as author K. P. Yohannan wrote, "The trouble with half-truths is that they contain within them full lies."[4]

Stop feeding your teenage girl the "It doesn't matter what other people think about you" lie. It's not fair to her—she can't help but gobble it up. Adolescent girls can hardly wait to reject the expectations and judgments placed on them by an unforgiving society. They refuse to sacrifice their rights as free citizens just because someone somewhere doesn't approve! They are leading the charge to free us all from social slavery! At least that's what they think they're doing. But the reality is less kicking-tails-and-taking-names and more stupidly-shooting-oneself-in-the-foot.

> Relationships matter, reputations matter, testimonies matter. Girls should care what other people think about them. #10things

Relationships matter, reputations matter, testimonies matter. Girls should care what other people think about them.

Chronic Overcorrectors

History repeats itself. We are always discovering a new way of doing things that is really an old way of doing things. In parenting: babies should sleep on their stomachs; no, their backs; no, their stomachs. In nutrition: butter is healthier; no, margarine is healthier; no, it's definitely butter. In religion: we should focus on discipleship; no, evangelism; no, discipleship.

We humans are chronic overcorrectors. We swing wide one way, then the other—each generation trying to compensate for the weaknesses of our parents, each revealing weaknesses of our own. Back and forth, back and forth, through the ages.

C. S. Lewis used to say that for every current book he read, he'd read a really old book. The reason, he said, was that we are prone to chronological snobbery. As in, "It's newer, therefore it is more relevant. The way we do things now is better, smarter, and more efficient than the way our parents (and grandparents) did things."

I think about this a lot at church when I hear things like "This is not your grandparents' church." "We aren't afraid to be real." "We believe in engaging the culture." "We believe in community and doing life together." As if my generation invented authenticity. Like all the Christians who came before us for hundreds of years loved hypocrisy and judgment and nobody before us ever thought of using the New Testament church as a model.

Every time I consider our world, Scripture proves itself right again: "There is nothing new under the sun" (Eccl. 1:9).

A few generations ago, the advice, "Your reputation matters; you should care what people think of you" hardly needed to be said. People would have looked at you and said, "Duh," because that is the kind of thing people said a few generations ago. At the time, people lived in smaller, rural communities. The Internet didn't exist. Verbal agreements were binding. Your word was your bond. You shook on things.

But when we are left to our own devices, we take things too far. I'm sure it started with a few overachieving

Type A's who were all, "I'm going to win at caring what people think!" What started out as building a good name within a community (which is wise), devolved into finding self-worth in what others thought (which is damaging)—and everything got all messed up.

People became chronic people-pleasers.

They were afraid to say "no."

All criticism felt like a personal attack.

People felt overwhelming pressure to conform.

People put as much stock in a stranger's opinion of them as they did in what they knew to be true of themselves.

An entire generation of young women spent their best years haunted by the words, "But what will people think?" As they matured, they saw the unnecessary burden they'd been carrying around all those years; they understood that the obsession with what other people thought was the root of their crippling insecurity and shame. So they vowed never to place that same burden on their daughters. They whispered to their little girls as they tucked them in at night, "It doesn't matter what anybody else thinks about you; you are beautiful." They comforted them through middle school rumors and high school drama, "It doesn't matter what anybody else thinks about you; you know what's true." And they said proudly at graduation celebrations, "Don't dwell on what everyone else thinks; you can accomplish anything you set your mind to."

It is no surprise that the next generation of young women held high the banner of "It doesn't matter what anybody thinks about me!" Their parents weren't crazy; the ability to weed out unhelpful opinions is healthy. It is essential to realizing our worth. It is helpful in doing what's right, even when it's not popular—for standing up for what we believe in. It is crucial in order to foster any kind of creativity. But in our zeal we take it too far. The girls who were taught not to care what people thought about them overcorrected, and are living with a set of consequences they never saw coming.

They sacrificed relationships with their parents because they didn't care what they thought.

They uncensored themselves. They voiced rude and gossipy remarks under the guise of "I don't care what anyone thinks; I'm just telling the truth."

They became increasingly egocentric. Their own opinions were the only standard for their behavior.

They dismissed advice (and often common sense) because there was no reason to listen; it only mattered what they thought anyway. Outside opinions about their choices were irrelevant.

Friendships ended unnecessarily because they chose being "true to themselves" over reconciliation and compromise. They became islands unto themselves, worshipping independence and personal conviction.

In short, they are lonely. Also, they might have an ill-advised Tweety Bird tattoo (as all Tweety Bird tattoos are) because "What do my parents know? Of course I won't regret it. I can make adult decisions on my own!" The irony of Tweety Bird tattoos representing mature adult decisions is not lost on me.

Adolescence is the season of boundary pushing. It is self-discovery and unfurling tiny wings and leaping out of nests. Teenagers are especially susceptible to the lure of "I don't care what anybody thinks of me" because it suits them. It is the perfect sentiment on which to build any argument. If you object to the clothes she wants to wear, the company she keeps, or the swill she overshares on the Internet, all she has to do is proclaim, "But it doesn't matter what anyone else thinks about me!"

If you've been feeding her that line since her childhood, you have nowhere to go from there. Anything you say is backpedalling, so you'll just stand there, floundering, mouth agape like a trout.

We've been using the phrase "It doesn't matter what anybody else thinks about you" to teach girls self-confidence for so long that they've started regurgitating it right back at us like little birds, using it to make their rebellion sound noble instead of foolhardy.

"I'm going to get this face tattoo and if my boss has a problem with it, then she's shallow and cares too much about appearances."

"If Suzy thinks I'm a snob then she doesn't have to hang out with me anymore, nobody's forcing her. I know I'm a nice person and that's what matters."

"I'm going to take the job at Hooters even though my parents don't want me to. I need a job and don't care what anyone thinks about me."

As idealistic as it sounds, that kind of reasoning is shortsighted, self-centered, and immature.

Remember maturity? It is not "a vague philosophical concept, but a trained ability to meet the demands of reality." I am so completely serious about requiring teenagers to memorize this definition. Welcome to the real world, kiddos. Put on your big girl pants and repeat after me:

Not getting a face tattoo isn't conformist; it's mature.

Caring what Suzy thinks (and honoring her thoughts and preferences over your own for the sake of a friendship) isn't weak; it's mature.

Being nice to someone you don't like isn't hypocritical; it's mature.

Keeping your mouth shut isn't cowardly; it's mature.

Accepting criticism and using it to grow isn't letting other people define you; it's being mature.

I have no doubt that people will take the advice "Your reputation matters; you should care what others think of you" too far. They'll swing wide like so many generations before them and run themselves ragged, threadbare, trying to get everybody to like them. They'll make themselves crazy thinking about it, and that will be a tragedy.

We're overcorrectors. We are kids on a balance beam, just trying to get from one side of life to the other uninjured and unembarrassed. We wobble one way, then the other, trying to find a balance that's sustainable—a way of living that will get us to the other side without all the violent back and forth. No whiplash and no regrets: that's the goal.

> We are kids on a balance beam, just trying to get from one side of life to the other uninjured and unembarrassed. #10things

I believe the balance is grace.

Grace for ourselves. What others think doesn't define me.

Grace for others. Their opinions are valid; I'll listen graciously.

Grace for everyone.

There is no other way.

Dumb Is Never Cute

*"Above all, be the heroine of your own life,
not the victim."*
NORA EPHRON[1]

*"You are a woman with a brain and reasonable
ability. Stop whining and find something to do."*
DOWAGER COUNTESS OF GRANTHAM,
DOWNTON ABBEY[2]

*"We have to declare a princess-free zone. No tiaras,
no Girls Gone Wild, no pretending we can't carry
things. No fairy tales, no waiting around to be
rescued, and absolutely no playing dumb."*
SHAUNA NIEQUIST[3]

Women have come a long way.

If I had been born in the Jianxgi province of China in the year 2000, there's a good chance I would have been aborted when my parents discovered I was a girl. If I'd been born in India, it's not likely that I would have been taught to read or write. If I'd been born in Saudi Arabia, I would need permission from my male guardian to travel or receive an education. If I'd been born in the Democratic Republic of Congo, I would have had a 22 percent chance of being sexually abused. If I'd been born in the United States before 1920, I would not have been able to vote, because at the time a woman's opinion on matters of country was irrelevant. Until the 19th Amendment was ratified, 50 percent of the population was muted, politically speaking, because of our gender and its implicit roles.

Indeed, women, across all cultures, have come a very long way.

Even so, female CEOs and Supreme Court justices, like Facebook's Sheryl Sandburg and Justice Ruth Bader Ginsburg, are still overcoming prejudices that peg women as overly emotional, indecisive, and only passable at math, mechanical, and leadership skills. These women at the top of their fields are fighting hard, even now, to demonstrate that women are not ruled by their sympathies (or their hormones), that they can be an integral part of any team, and that they can lead well.

Teenage girls would do well to remember the world into which they were born a woman, and to remember the worlds into which they, mercifully, were not. Thanks to the tenacity of women that have gone before, our girls are as likely, if not more likely, to be accepted into college as their male counterparts. Female leaders exist in virtually every field. There are female surgeons, film directors, lawyers, executives, comedians, entrepreneurs, astronauts, pilots, and professional athletes. Growing up, today's teenage girls believe that they can be anything—and their generation is one of the first that could dare to think so.

The world is vast and big and bright for teenage girls—and too many women have worked too hard to see women esteemed for girls to act like a bunch of flirtatious twits to get what they want.

The Price

A double standard exists in the minds of too many women that goes something like this: if a man manipulates a woman—if he romances her to get what he wants, at work or otherwise—he's a pig. But if a woman manipulates a man, she was just using her feminine wiles—a tool in her arsenal, to get what was coming to her.

I'm surprised by how many women believe that the flippant manipulation of men is within the parameters of womanhood, and at how early this mindset takes root. I see it in girls citing PMS to get out of gym class (girls for whom PMS isn't excruciating cramps, but a measly handful of dates on a calendar). I see it in girls using their cleavage to get out of speeding tickets, flirting to procure information, and exaggerating frailty to get others to do the heavy lifting. I've heard women banter with each other, saying things like, "I can get whatever I want from my boyfriend," or "I'm not ashamed that I flirt to get favors—I can!" They're laughing, but they're not joking.

I suppose I get it; I get that control makes a woman feel powerful, and empowerment is like a Starbucks blueberry scone: once you have it you wonder how you ever lived without it, and there is absolutely no turning back. (I've heard this is true of other, more dangerous substances too, but I'm speaking of what I know.) I understand that eliciting a desired response from a man makes women feel beautiful and unstoppable—the very things that the men they care the most deeply about don't make them feel often enough. The whole thing is very practical. It works, as long as the ends justify the means.

But I want to call attention to the logical end of this thinking. Whether women are manipulating out of presumed entitlement or of pure practicality, they are manipulating to their own detriment.

It's difficult for a woman to insist that PMS doesn't handicap her decision-making or her emotional stability when she's been using it to justify every lazy impulse and emotional lashing out since the sixth grade.

A woman can't flirt her way to the top and then be surprised when someone accuses her of not having the chops to do the job. She can't be offended at the insinuation that she doesn't have the work ethic if she's never actually shown anyone her work ethic. "Work ethic" is not synonymous with "coy conversational undertones." They both work, but they aren't the same, so we can't expect the same outcomes.

This kind of behavior is a bait and switch; it's like saying, "Look at how fabulous my lips are! Look how pouty and enticing. I am laughing at all of your jokes with my perfectly glossed lips that, by now, you are thinking about kissing. You should keep me around and happy so that I will keep pouting my flirty lips at you." And then, in the very next breath saying, "How dare you say that I only got this job because of my lips!?"

This kind of stunt is how women get reputations as snakes. It doesn't mean they aren't qualified,

Sisters, we either show the world that we have brains, passions, and skills—or we don't. We can't have it both ways. #10things

but how could anyone possibly know? Sisters, we either show the world that we have brains, passions, and skills—or we don't. We can't have it both ways.

Of course we can bat our eyelashes, show a little skin, and giggle our way into a job, into a man's heart, or into the spotlight. But at what cost?

The cost of being an ego-stroker first and a talent second—once you get there—is inadvertently teaching girls that it's okay to manipulate other people. The cost is inadvertently communicating that ego-stroking is what women have to do to be successful, or at least, it's what you had to do. The elite group of people who have risked life and limb to climb Mount Everest aren't impressed by someone who helicopters to the top. It's not where you are that counts; it's how you got there. If you don't have standards on the way up, you can't claim to have them when you arrive—wherever it is you're going. You won't lose your skill, but you will lose your credibility. Once you start batting eyelashes, eyelashes is all you've got.

That price is too high. My own credibility, the esteem of women and the way they think and work, is not something I'm willing to sacrifice on the altar of "but it's so easy."

If you believe that suggestive flirting and damsel-in-distress-ing is just a way to level the playing field, you gravely underestimate yourself and the strength and intelligence of the female race. The only thing required to level the playing field is for the girls in the arena to break out the big guns: passion, skill, education, and well-reasoned opinions.

You are not a twit; so don't act like one because you think it serves you. It's a short-term perk with an ugly underbelly; it's a trap. It's easy to feel like you've won when you can get whatever you want, but when you realize you've been objectified or patronized, it doesn't feel much like winning anymore. No matter what you get in the end (fame, fortune, a promotion at work, the guy of your dreams, or a discount at the mechanic), if you've been objectified along the way, it's not a win. It's a big, fat loss for women everywhere.

The Richard Simmons of Prayer: On Living at Point M

Femininity is a superpower, not a one-trick pony. I want women to work their femininity in all of its glorious whole-ness, not prostitute it, offering their bodies up for enjoyment (physically or mentally) in unspoken agreements in exchange for what they want. If you think this is just the way the world works, you may be right—but I submit that we change that. I submit that we start living our ideals instead of our practicalities.

When I was in high school, I went on a mission trip every summer to Tijuana, Mexico, and San Diego, California. Our team ran Vacation Bible Schools to support churches and orphanages in Mexico, and we attended an apologetics and evangelism conference in California. As a part of the conference, each student was to spend a day in prayer and fasting. There was a contingent of students that stayed on campus each day to be guided in prayer by one of the conference leaders named Paul. Five minutes into my day of prayer I knew— this was an experience that I had no category for. My comfort zone was obliterated. Paul was expressive and uninhibited. There was lots of singing and shouting and crying out, lots of clapping and extending of arms. Paul used language I'd only heard in televangelist sermons. Halfway through the day we went on a prayer walk, and while we were en route, my friend leaned in and whispered to me, "Kate, he's like the Richard Simmons of Prayer!"

I am here to tell you that you can pray and laugh at the same time, because I did—for the next six hours. I think at one point he may have shouted, "I'm a pony! I'm a pony!" When we debriefed with our team at the end of the day, I told my youth pastor's wife about my experience. She laughed with me, then told me something I've never forgotten. She said, "Sometimes we need someone down at Point M to help us move from Point A to Point B."

The Richard Simmons of Prayer changed the way I pray. He taught me that I could fast and pray all day and never grow bored. Weary, but never bored. He taught me about living in constant communication with God, about how to approach the throne boldly in my time of need, about how reverence looks, and about how to listen—how to speak with God, not just at Him. My expression in worship and prayer changed because of the Richard Simmons of Prayer. I began to understand how inextricably the physical is connected to the spiritual. I moved from A to B.

That is advocacy—living at Point M (likely labeled excessive and fanatical) to draw people toward the truth you believe in, a truth so big it's worth advocating. Advocates live at Point M, obliterating comfort zones, moving everyone around them from A to B.

I am willing to live down at Point M for our girls. I am willing to adopt a zero-tolerance policy for flirting for gain. I am willing to be called cold, and prudish, and a buzz-kill. I believe that women manipulating men (by flirtation or any other means) isn't as innocuous as our culture suggests. I believe that it is damaging to the cause of women. Moreover, I believe that, gender issues aside, people manipulating other people is never okay. We must stop teaching our girls that dumb is cute.

Don't be a twit; be better than that. Don't undermine yourself and, for crying out loud, don't undermine me. Adopt a zero-tolerance policy on manipulation. Why are we so afraid to do this? It's not unrealistic and it won't make us cold; it will make us sincere. You have nothing to lose unless the whole of your feminine charm is found in your ability to play princess. I don't understand the hesitation; are men afraid that no woman will want to flirt with them sincerely? Are women so cold that, were we to eliminate empty flattery, we would have nothing left to praise? Speak the truth in love; encourage each other while the day is called today; kind words are like honey, sweet to the soul and health to the body— these are the truths of Jesus. So be a light! Encourage others liberally, be generous with praise; lavish it on those around you. Be warm and charming and sincere. Love people well—and know that in so doing, there is no room for manipulation.

> Love people well—and know that in so doing, there is no room for manipulation. #10things

Adopt a zero-tolerance policy for twit-dom; do it to create a better space for the girls we are raising. I look into the face of my five-year-old, my darling Madeline, who asks me questions about her small intestine and Neptune and atoms and the omnipresence of God, my girl who is socially skilled and exceptionally nurturing, and I know I must carry the torch that has been passed to me by the women who've gone before. The women who did hard things, who perhaps didn't achieve what they could have by flirting, and in so doing achieved even more.

I am calling for mothers and grandmothers and teachers and mentors to carry their torches too.

I am calling for strong women. Not androgynous women. Not harsh, shrill, or prudish women. I'm calling for beautiful, gentle, compassionate, women—with spines and wills of steel. I'm calling for women who know their value, their intelligence, and their skill, and behave accordingly.

How Not to Be a Twit

Here are nine ways for girls to ensure that they don't damage their reputations by acting like twits. Teach them to your teenage girl in word and deed.

1. Don't use femininity as a cop-out. Don't fake frailty where frailty doesn't exist. Don't claim biology when biology isn't a factor. Don't manipulate people. Don't play dumb.

2. Know thyself—and set yourself up for success accordingly. If you know that you get a little sensitive or emotional for a few days each month, be aware of that. There is no shame in it—zero—but make sure that you give your body the rest, nutrition, and breathing room it needs.

3. Don't assume sexism. If you are passed over for a promotion or someone does you the kindness of offering to help, don't assume sexism. Just ask yourself how you can be better. You can't cite your femininity as a liability while insisting that others don't do the same. And don't operate with a chip on your shoulder; it's not becoming. Not every knock is discrimination.

4. Accept help. Strong women know that it is wise to accept help. When I urge women not to play helpless or coy, I'm not talking about accepting help or chivalry; I am The Queen of accepting chivalry. Open my door? Yes, please. Take my car to get it detailed? Thank you very much. Pay for my dinner? I'll have the Ahi tuna steak—*and* dessert. I'll also take your coat because I'm chilly, and I want to be the first off of a sinking ship. Accepting chivalry and help doesn't demean or take advantage of men; manipulation does, and therein lies a world of difference. In fact, accepting chivalry esteems men. I make no bones about the fact that my husband has come to my rescue a thousand times in a thousand ways. I love him, I need him, and I feel safe when he takes care of me. There is no weakness in that; there is love in that.

I'm not talking about accepting help, either. I need people to help me with the heavy lifting, literally and figuratively. Life is hard, and we are in it together. We carry each other through and sometimes we carry each other's couches and refrigerators and boxes of books.

If you don't accept help when you really need it, you're going to end up looking like a twit anyway because you're going to fail—or drop a box of books on your head.

I need people to help me with the heavy lifting, literally and figuratively. Life is hard, and we are in it together. #10things

Accept help; it makes you humble and gracious; it makes you human, and a friend.

5. Work hard. Be creative. Take risks. Keep learning. Teach yourself to set goals that make people raise their eyebrows and say, "Wow!"

6. Build appropriate relationships. Relationships matter; networking is not the same thing as manipulating. Allies are different from flirting pawns. All movement in life, corporate and otherwise, is about who you know and how well they like you. Reputation matters (this is why you don't want your reputation to be that of a twit). Be a friend, find a mentor, be a mentor.

7. Be confident. Assume you can. Do things that scare you.

8. Don't lose your femininity. You are a woman, don't lose sight of that! Femininity is a superpower. We don't need androgynous leaders, we need female leaders.

Use your feminine strengths; plan for your feminine weaknesses. Be unashamedly, uninhibitedly womanly.

9. Be your truest self. If you love something, dare to really love it—unapologetically and without disclaimers, in a totally nerdy way. Author John Green wrote, "Nerds like us are allowed to be unironically enthusiastic about stuff. Nerds are allowed to love stuff—like jump-up-and-down-in-your-chair-can't-control-yourself love it. When people call people nerds, mostly what they're saying is, 'You like stuff,' which is not a great insult at all. Like, 'You are too enthusiastic about the miracle of human consciousness.'"[4] Amy Poehler challenges girls to change the world by being themselves; she says it this way, "When you are interested in something, your life becomes more interesting and you become more interesting. Caring is cool."[5] Be yourself without reservation. If you feel strongly about something, stick to your guns. If you believe in something, advocate for it. Fill the void that only you can fill by being the person only you can be—you.

Chapter 10

Enough

"Always be a first-rate version of yourself instead of a second-rate version of somebody else."
JUDY GARLAND[1]

"Be yourself. Everyone else is already taken."
OSCAR WILDE[2]

"Let me know that You hear me
Let me know Your touch.
Let me know that You love me
And let that be enough."
SWITCHFOOT[3]

I studied advertising in college. I paid a good sum of money (which I will be repaying until the day I die or until the rapture, whichever comes first), for a communications degree with a double specialization in advertising and public relations. I worked in marketing for exactly three months before I moved states, found out I was pregnant, and stayed home to raise my babies. If the point of college had been the degree it would have been a colossal waste of time and money. Good thing the point wasn't the degree—it was the education. I've used the education every day since. I've used it in my marriage, my ministry, my parenting, and my writing. Plus I met my husband in college, so I'll go to my grave insisting it was worth every penny, DAD.

What I know about advertising is that one of the primary objectives is to create need where need does not exist. In order for you to buy something, you have to believe that you need it. You need it because it's useful, because it will save you time or effort. You need it because it's convenient, or prestigious. You need it because it will make you happy, or pretty. You need it to wear to work, or to the gym. You need it because it's delicious, or healthy. You need it so that your mother-in-law will approve. You need it because you want it, or because you're worth it. You need it because it's on sale, because you'll never find it this cheap again. Every ad, every slogan, every campaign is designed to make you feel like you need this thing—over the absence of it and over every other product or brand.

Another thing I know is that any product with a television commercial isn't a necessity. There are no commercials for bread, bananas, school uniforms, or tap water. You never see a commercial for a modest, one-bedroom home. The commercial is for a real estate agency, and it features stately, upper-middle class homes and a Realtor driving a Benz. You need a home; they create need for the "American Dream."

There are no commercials for basic soap. The commercials are for body washes and shaving gels that are guaranteed to nourish forty-seven layers of skin and also get you a tall, fit, well-dressed, hygienic, football player for a boyfriend while it's at it. You need soap; they create need for sensual soap.

If you really need a thing, there's no point in advertising because you're going to buy it anyway. Tina Fey says it this way, "When people say, 'You really, really must' do something, it means you don't really have to. No one ever says, 'You really, really must deliver the baby during labor.' When it's true, it doesn't need to be said."[4]

Companies know that the only way to get you to buy the upper-middle class home and the get-a-boyfriend body wash is to make you believe that you need it.

I recently saw a Crest commercial wherein a very attractive man sees his ex-girlfriend and does a double take because she's laughing with a huge, ear-to-ear, Julia Roberts kind of smile and her teeth are so white. Then he walks over and starts flirting with her because her teeth are so white. The implicit message is that the handsome man regrets breaking up with his girlfriend because now her teeth are so white.

In what kind of weird alternate universe is this a plausible scenario? Did he break up with her because her teeth weren't white enough? Are the teeth a metaphor for her personality? This is the only thing I can figure, because I'm pretty sure I could whiten all the livelong day and none of my exes are going to come banging on the door to grovel.

Axe products are another terrible offender. The slogan for their shampoo is "Get some hair action," and it is accompanied by scantily clad older women running their fingers through a pimply, middle school boy's hair. This is creating need on an expert level. You know that every boy that sees their commercial is all, "Mom, I need this shampoo. No, you don't understand. I NEED it."

To create need: this is the agenda of every ad in existence.

> You won't get the job without this breath mint.
>
> You won't get the hair without this shampoo.
>
> You won't get the status without this car.
>
> You won't get the guy without this teeth-whitening cream.

This agenda is what makes the beauty industry so dangerous to young women. In order for a company to create need in a girl where it did not previously exist, they must create in her a dissatisfaction with the current state of affairs—a dissatisfaction with herself.

The ugly truth about advertising is that the self-images of little girls are collateral damage—an unfortunate, but acceptable consequence in the bigger picture of industry growth. Hear me: the beauty industry is not the enemy. The people in the advertising industry don't hate women, and they are most certainly not out to decimate the egos of our children. In fact, many of them are feminists, working hard to empower the next generation of young women. But the fact remains: every single day she's alive, your teenage girl is exposed to hundreds of messages intentionally designed to make her unhappy with herself.

What's worse, we must consider frequency in addition to the constancy of the message. Teenage girls are surrounded by advertising every minute of every day: online, on their phones, at school, in every store window and on every rack of clothing, on television, in movies, and in magazines. This means that every minute of every day they are receiving messages that say, "You need

> Every minute of every day they are receiving messages that say, "You need improving and your as-is self is not enough."
> #10things

improving and your as-is self is not enough." It is a bombardment, an onslaught.

Their universes imply:

You are not thin enough. Your skin is not tan enough, or light enough, depending on your ethnicity. What we're really saying is that your skin is not latte-colored and racially nondescript, like someone who is Latin or Middle Eastern. But God forbid you look discernibly Latin or Middle Eastern, because that's no good either. Your teeth are not white enough or straight enough. Also, your breath will never be fresh enough.

Your skin is not young, firm, smooth, tight, hydrated, or pore-less enough. You don't look airbrushed enough. (No one ever seems to stop and ask, "Does anybody?")

Your legs are not long enough, and your thighs touch. (There is a huge collective of women whose biggest concern about their bodies is that their thighs touch.) Your legs are not smooth enough, and while we're at it, neither are your armpits. (Does anyone else think it unreasonable that prickle on a woman's legs is such a scarlet letter? My prickle happens in like an hour and a half. I used to spend an hour shaving, bringing my total shower time to seventy minutes because I thought if I pressed hard enough, was thorough enough, my legs would stay smoother longer. It took me years to make peace with the fact that I am not made of synthetic plastic; I am human—made of flesh and blood and hair and

I should stop wasting my time in the shower despairing over the rate of return on my leg hair. Whatever, man, I shaved. I did my part. That's all anyone can ask of me.)

You are not tall enough. You are too tall. You don't have enough curves. You are pear shaped; we have Spanx for that.

Your toes are too long and your heels are too rough. Your lips are not pouty enough, or shiny enough, or outlined enough. Your eyelashes are not long, dark, thick, or curvy enough. (Do our eyelashes really need to be all those things?)

Your stomach is not flat enough. Your rear end is not curvy enough. Your breasts are not big enough, or perky enough. (Never mind that it defies the laws of physics to have breasts that are both large and perky.)

Your nails are not strong enough. Your hands are not soft enough. Your hair is not long enough, shiny enough, silky enough, straight enough, curly enough, thick enough, or voluminous enough. You are not stylish enough, modern enough, hipster enough, classy enough, popular enough, or wealthy enough.

Then these companies say, "Here, let us help. We can fix you."

Except, no. They can't.

These messages program us for dissatisfaction at best, and at worst, they program us to really, sincerely believe that we are so flawed and undesirable that we are unworthy of romance, friendship, respect, or love. It is the great mercy of God that any of us are even remotely well-adjusted.

In this sense, it is each girl against the world. It is your beautiful, eager-to-please girl looking up into the face of a looming tsunami. It is all the dollars in all the pockets of all the executives versus your girl. Who could survive that? How will our girls survive it?

————

From my childhood and into my twenties, I suffered from uncharacteristically high self-esteem. Sure, I was jealous of other girls because everyone is jealous of other girls, but I largely believed that I had it going on. My body image took a small dip after my first and second babies, and went into an all-out tailspin after my third, but even now I find shades, whispers, of my high self-esteem of yore. For example, after the birth of each of my children I go shopping for postpartum clothes. I pick up a pair of shorts that I just know will fit, and when I get to the dressing room, I literally cannot get them over my thighs. This is not an exaggeration; I have to move up three sizes from where I start, every time. This makes postpartum shopping even more depressing than it already is, which—if you've ever been postpartum shopping—you know it is very hard to do. Even today I believe myself to be three sizes smaller than I actually am. I give myself the benefit of the doubt; my default setting is to believe that my clothes are fitting well, my hair is falling fabulously, and my skin is looking great. I believe this so unswervingly that I am often jarred by my own reflection in store windows and bathroom mirrors. I catch a glimpse of myself and think, *Wait, what? No way! This thing must be distorted, because I know I look better than this lady staring back at me.* All the cameras are liars; I believe that.

Because of my better-than-average body image (and without much introspection), I assumed that I never struggled with self-esteem—that I had somehow been spared the constant striving and measuring up that tortured so many of my peers.

This illusion came crashing down one night during my senior year of college. That year, I lived with a vague, overarching sense of desperation. It was like a fine mist of anxiety that touched both everything and nothing. On the second night of my spring break I sat on my bed—reading and journaling. I was reflecting on my relationships, and considering my spiritual and emotional state when I had an epiphany. These words materialized on my page:

> "I want someone to <u>enjoy</u> taking care of me. I want to be worth it."

The word "enjoy" is underlined, and the whole page is smattered with teardrops.

I stared at the words for a moment. Then, it was as if the levies that had been holding back the cumulative fears of twenty-one years burst. For the first time, I felt what had been there all along, nagging from just below the surface of my consciousness. The inadequacy was crushing; it knocked the wind out of me. The fear was acute, piercing. I felt the striving fully, agonizingly. I recognized entire facets of my personality as the behaviors of a girl trying to squeeze herself into everything a young woman should be: confident, friendly, a good conversationalist. Independent, not needy; only a joy, never a burden. Cute, flirtatious, beautiful, intelligent, and demure.

My insecurities were (and are) more social than physical: I need too much, I feel too much, I am too quiet, I am too shy, it is hard to know me, I am not worth the trouble it takes, I am not enough.

I felt as if my heart had curled up into the fetal position, tiny, tight, and cramping. I sat there on my childhood bed, looking and feeling very much like a little girl, and I wept. I said to God, "You take care of me; You enjoy taking care of me" over and over, until I almost believed it.

Those same tired insecurities are still hanging around, but I recognize them now, so they don't knock the wind out of me anymore. As an adult, what I want more than anything is for someone to tell me, at the end of every wearisome day, "You've done enough."

As an adult, I know that the "not enough" message isn't exclusive to teenage girls or to women who've birthed three children. It isn't specific to body image, and it is no respecter of persons. The most beautiful, self-assured, powerful, productive woman longs to hear, at the end of every long day, "You did enough today. It is okay to breathe now. You are enough."

> The most beautiful, self-assured, powerful, productive woman longs to hear, at the end of every long day, "You did enough today. It is okay to breathe now. You are enough."
> #10things

The Scales

Imagine a scale. On one side are all the messages of affirmation and sufficiency a teenage girl receives in a week: a daily "I love you" from Mom, a church service, a girl-power song on the radio. On the other side, imagine the messages of insufficiency a teenage girl receives in a week: a gushing fire hydrant of ads designed to create need, an onslaught of images of women that have been

Photoshopped within an inch of their lives. The high school caste system, and social media likes and follows—a cruelly quantifiable measure of popularity.

The imbalance is staggering. It makes me angry. It makes me sad—to think of all the women who have been tortured by self-hatred every time they dress, undress, shop, shower, or pass a mirror. It makes me feel compassion; I recognize the behaviors of so many teenage girls (immodesty, flirtation, drama, eating disorders, cutting) as their very best efforts to reconcile what they are with what they feel they need to be. It makes me desperate for my beautiful, perfect daughter to know that she is beautiful—that she is valuable, and enough. And it motivates me; we must fix the imbalance—right this ship.

The solution to the imbalance isn't balance. If a scale is tipped and you add equal measure to both sides, it stays tipped. The solution to imbalance is counterbalance. We don't just tell our girls they are beautiful. We don't just tell them they're good. We wage war.

And the message we take to the front lines is, "You are enough." It is the epitaph on our banners, the crest on our shields, our battle hymn.

This radical message of sufficiency, of intrinsic value and worth, is the only truth that carries enough weight to tip the scales of self-worth. No attack on the beauty industry will make a girl respect her body. Flattery and clichés are lightweights. You could pile thousands of

"You are beautiful to me," and "It doesn't matter what anyone else thinks about you," and "You're perfect just the way you are" onto the scale and it wouldn't amount to a heap of feathers.

The reason "You're perfect just the way you are" isn't reassuring to women (and isn't connecting with teenage girls) is because it's not true—and we know it. The reason it doesn't make us feel better is because we know better. We know too much of our own flaws and broken places to be persuaded that we're perfect just the way we are, no matter how enthusiastically anyone insists. Platitudes don't heal hearts; truth does.

We are tired, short-tempered, pimpled, anxious, selfish, envious, insecure, gossipy, frizzy-haired, prickly-legged creatures. We can never believe ourselves perfect—but maybe, just maybe, if someone tells us often enough, if someone loves us steadfastly enough, we could dare to believe that we are enough.

We are enough because God declares us so. This is the great scandal of the gospel.

> We are enough because God declares us so. This is the great scandal of the gospel. #10things

God invented justice. He hates evil more than we, in our moral indignation and human self-righteousness, could dream. He banished Lucifer to hell for his blasphemous pride. God knows that the wages of sin is death, and He requires the shedding of blood for the remission of sins. He is utterly holy, perfectly pure.

We lie and cheat and steal. We are filthy, tainted by our prejudices and our selfishness. We are ungrateful, lustful, lazy, and idolatrous. With our minutes, hours, and dollars we idolize our jobs, schedules, families, comforts—even our own bodies. Imperfect is a weak euphemism; we are abhorrent.

A just God and a sin-sick people have no business engaging in a great love affair, but we are. Tim Keller wrote, "You are more sinful than you could dare imagine, and you are more loved and accepted than you could ever dare hope."[5] The gospel is scandalous. God doesn't love us because we are enough—we are enough because He loves us. We are enough to be loved radically. We are enough to be pursued, ransomed, redeemed, bought back, sacrificed for, rejoiced in, cleansed, purified—worked on and in and through. We are not perfect, but He is perfecting us.

Enough Internally

God doesn't look at the things people look at. "Man looks at the outward appearance, but the LORD looks at the heart" (1 Sam. 16:7). Seeing as God knows the exact number of hairs on my head right now, I'm sure He sees my prickly legs too. But the jet-black prickles on my porcelain white legs are not a factor in my worth; they are completely irrelevant to my enoughness, thank God.

God is only concerned with the temporal as it relates to the eternal. He cares about my body as it pertains to my health, my self-discipline, my self-respect, my modesty, and my self-worth. The rest is neutral. He cares about the way your living room is decorated only to the degree that it reflects your spiritual condition: if you overspent, that matters. If you use it to entertain, love, grow children well, that matters. If you tend to it in such a way that allows you to be grateful and peaceful and happy, that matters. Beyond that, it's neutral, so don't fret so much about it. God is only ever concerned with what matters; He never needs a perspective shift. He IS the big picture. He IS wisdom. He IS the truth. And the thing that God cares about, the thing He looks at, is hearts.

> God is only ever concerned with what matters; He never needs a perspective shift. #10things

God cares not one iota about my prickles or the bags under my eyes. He is concerned with whether I pursued Him or my coffee more zealously this morning.

There is this incredible story in the New Testament where some guys brought Jesus a man that was paralyzed and lying on a mat. Jesus rewarded their faith by telling the man, "Your sins are forgiven"—because He knew that the man's biggest problem wasn't his legs; it was his heart. Of course, everyone around thinks Jesus is (1) blasphemous, (2) crazy, and (3) a little bit of a jerk for not healing the guy, if He can in fact heal people. And get this:

> Knowing their thoughts, Jesus said, "Why do you entertain evil thoughts in your hearts? Which is easier: to say, 'Your sins are forgiven,' or to say, 'Get up and walk'? But so that you may know that the Son of Man has authority on earth to forgive sins. . . ." Then he said to the paralytic, "Get up, take your mat and go home." And the man got up and went home. When the crowd saw this, they were filled with awe; and they praised God, who had given such authority to men. (Matt. 9:4–8)

Jesus did a physical miracle to demonstrate His authority, to get us to consider: Which is more difficult to deal with—paralysis or sin? Which matters more—legs or souls? The obvious answer is implicit: souls, hearts. This is what matters to God. Nobody had to die for God to heal paralytics, but someone had to pay in blood for the sins of the world; perfect justice requires it. No wrong can be overlooked; no one is off the hook. The redemption of our souls is why Jesus came; all the healing was just to get our attention.

And so, if God, in His omniscience and holy zeal, sees all my ugliness of heart and still declares me enough, why should I ever despair? If He can handle my sin, how much more can He handle my baby weight? God tells us that "physical training is of some value, but godliness has value for all things, holding promise for both the present life and the life to come" (1 Tim. 4:8). He tells us that our "beauty should not come from outward adornment, such as braided hair and the wearing of gold jewelry and fine clothes. Instead, it should be that of your inner self, the unfading beauty of a gentle and quiet spirit, which is of great worth in God's sight" (1 Pet. 3:3–4). Anne Lamott says, "Joy is the best makeup."[6] I know people like this, people who glow, and one of my highest ambitions in life is to become one. I want to have a beautiful spirit, to be gentle, to be described as kind.

It is our hearts that matter, and our hearts are loved. It is our souls that endure, and our souls are redeemed. The externals are neutral—temporary and fading fast (see Prov. 31:30). The inside is where our value lies, and our insides are enough.

Enough Eternally

We are enough to matter eternally. All the days ordained for us were written in His book before one of them came to be (see Ps. 139:16). When God breathed life into Adam's lungs, it was already written that we should live. Our eternal past existed in His mind and heart; we mattered. When we entered the world in our broken, sinful, bodies, the plan to rescue us was already in place—already in play: Jesus would pay the ransom for our souls. Our eternal future existed in His mind and heart; we mattered. God declared our worth at creation and affirmed it on the cross, leaving no room for doubt—we are doubly valuable: made and redeemed. Doubly loved: breathed and bought.

You are enough internally and eternally. You are enough, doubly, in every way that matters.

If your mother resented you, you are enough. If your father left you, you are enough. If your husband cheated on you, you are enough. If you have an addiction, you are enough. If you are depressed, you are enough.

You aren't perfect, but you are enough in every way that matters. Right now, in this freeze-frame. No tweaks, no change of clothes, no slapping on mascara or sucking in your belly or rubbing lotion over scaly parts. No groveling or confession or making amends required. You are enough to be loved, right now.

The end of *Good Will Hunting* is one of my favorite scenes in any movie that's ever been made. It's the scene where abused, hardened, hurting Matt Damon collapses into his therapist's arms and sobs, while his therapist says over and over, "It's not your fault. It's not your fault. It's not your fault." The emotion is thick—tangible. I weep for relief with him every time. Deep breath. Catharsis. It's not your fault.

I suspect that if a therapist were to take any given woman by the shoulders, if he were to look deep into her eyes and insist, "You are enough. You are enough. You are enough," she would collapse into his arms and weep. I suspect that her knees would give way, unable to stand up under the relief of it. I suspect that all of us would be undone as we, battered and bruised, climbed out from under the weight of all of the things we've been measuring ourselves against for our entire lives.

"You are enough." This is the truth with which we wage war on insecurity. This is how we fight for our girls. We tell them as many times as it takes for them to hear us. We speak it, shout it, whisper it, sing it, write it. We put it on our mirrors and doors and refrigerators; we put it in our cars and cubicles and in our daughter's lunchboxes (see Deut. 6:6–9). We memorize it and pray it over our girls. We leave it on their pillows (with the melanoma pamphlets). We blast them with it; we say it over and over until they dare to believe it. "You are enough."

This truth—the scandalous love of God that calls us beautiful and valuable and enough—will rescue them, and us, all over again.

Women need it. We who spend, plan, fret, flirt, binge, and purge like we have something to prove need it.

Men who strive to measure up to some false and unattainable standard of stoic, heroic masculinity need it. They are enough too.

Kids that don't quite fit into the spaces that the world has carved out for them—kids that communicate or learn or whose bodies work differently—need to know it.

People who are hurting, hiding, aching, and searching need to know it: you are enough. No more striving; there is nothing left to earn (see Eph. 2:8–9). You are accepted—loved.

And teenage girls need it. They need it to survive their march through the gauntlet, and it is a gauntlet; I know it because I lived it. I am living it. I'm having to practice what I preach—desperately, religiously coming to Jesus and letting Him remind me, "You are not perfect; I am perfecting you. You are loved, internally and eternally. You are enough." I've worked with teenage girls since I was one of them—every day for more than ten years, and if I believe anything unswervingly, it is that teenage girls need to know that they are enough. It will literally change their lives.

The appropriation of "enough" is the antidote for all the behaviors you are sick and tired of. She doesn't have to dress immodestly to garner attention from anyone because she is enough. She doesn't have to go tanning, use a hair relaxer, outcry on social media, or stir up drama because she is enough. She doesn't need to smoke, play dumb, or flirt her way into what she wants because she is enough. She doesn't need to date idiots, wilt under the pressure of her course load, wear a size two, or have five hundred followers on Instagram.

What she needs is Jesus.

When your teenage girl is sad and sickly with unrequited love, when the person she can't stop thinking about doesn't notice her, she can come to Jesus and be assured, "You're enough."

When her dream college (or her safety college) says no, she can come to Jesus and remember, "You're enough."

When she drops the ball, when she messes up in an irreversible way, when there are consequences, she can come to Jesus and hear, "You're enough."

If you only teach your teenage girl one thing, teach her to come to Jesus. And you come too.

When it's the end of your fiscal year and the e-mails never stop, when only you can do the job well, but you can't do it all, when you wonder how it is possible that you work with so many idiots, when you take your phone to bed more than you take your husband to bed, when you haven't been to the grocery store in three weeks, and all your plants are dead, and you literally can't remember the last time you washed your sheets—come to Jesus. When you are bleary-eyed and dead inside, come to the cross and listen, "You are enough."

> *If you only teach your teenage girl one thing, teach her to come to Jesus. And you come too. #10things*

When your four-year-old refers to the laundry pile in your room as "the clothes forest." (This actually happened.) When your entire life: mental, physical, and emotional is an obstacle course because there is not a cumulative two square feet of clean between your home, car, and yard. When your back aches because you are perpetually bent at a ninety-degree angle, attending to little people and their messes only to break even—or worse, when you wake up in the hole, already behind, buried in yesterday's messes with no hope of ever reaching the surface again. When you see a childless woman and you start to cry because you want her life so badly, but then you hate yourself for wanting it. When you are drowning in guilt and fear and stale Cheerios—come to Jesus. Let Him tell you, "You've done enough, child. You *are* enough."

Whether you are 15 or 115, it is never too late to throw off the shackles of "not enough." There is no expiration date on the truth. When an advertisement asks, "Is your skin too dry, oily, wrinkly, old, blotchy?" You can dare to say, "No." You can dare to believe that you don't need every fix for everything that is purportedly wrong with you.

If you want smoother hair, fine, but as you fire up the flat iron, remember, "You're enough." If you want to drop ten or twenty or eighty-five pounds, great. But with every step, every overhead press, every lunge, remember, "I'm enough." With every pound shed, "I'm enough." With every binge, "I'm enough." Every pound gained back, "I'm enough." Your value is not contingent upon your success in any area. Not one. Not faithfulness, not kindness, not goodness, not honesty, not skinny-ness or popularity. You have value because you are a person. You have value because God says you do. This is God's story; His love makes you enough.

It's never too late to be free. It is never too late to come to Jesus and let Him save you, redeem and perfect you. It is never too late to drink deeply of His grace. Come to Jesus and let Him tell you, "Be still, child.

You are loved, child. You matter, child. I am enough for you; you are enough for Me. Believe and rest. Breathe. Enough."

10 Things I Want to Tell Teenage Girls

March 25, 2012

1. If you choose to wear shirts that show off your breasts, you will attract boys. To be more specific, you will attract the kind of boys that like to look down girls' shirts. If you want to date a guy who likes to look at other girls' breasts and chase skirts, then great job; keep it up. *If you don't* want to date a guy who ogles at the breasts of other women, then maybe you should stop offering your own breasts up for the ogling. All attention is not equal. You think you want attention, but you don't. You want respect. All attention is not equal.

2. Don't go to the tanning bed. You'll thank me when you go to your high school reunion and you look like you've been airbrushed and then Photoshopped compared to the tanning bed train wrecks formerly known as classmates—well, at least next to the ones that haven't died from skin cancer.

3. When you talk about your friends "anonymously" on Facebook, we know exactly who you're talking about. People are smarter than you think they are. Stop posting passive-aggressive statuses about the myriad ways your friends disappoint you.

4. Newsflash: the number of times you say "I hate drama" is a pretty good indicator of how much you love drama. Nondramatic people don't feel the need to discuss all the drama they didn't start and aren't involved in.

5. "Follow your heart" is probably the worst advice ever.

6. Never let a man make you feel weak or inferior because you are an emotional being. Emotion is good; it is nothing to be ashamed of. Emotion makes us better—so long as it remains in its proper place: subject to truth and reason.

7. Smoking is not cool.

8. Stop saying things like, "I don't care what anyone thinks about me." First of all, that's not true. And second of all, if it is true, you need a perspective shift. Your reputation matters—greatly. You should care what people think of you.

9. Don't play coy or stupid or helpless to get attention. Don't pretend something is too heavy so that a boy will carry it for you. Don't play dumb to stroke someone's ego. Don't bat your eyelashes in exchange for attention and expect to be taken seriously, ever. You can't have it both ways. Either you show the world that you have a brain and passions and skills, or you don't. There are no damsels in distress managing corporations, running countries, or managing households. The minute you start batting eyelashes, eyelashes is all you've got.

10. You are beautiful. You are enough. The world we live in is twisted and broken and for your entire life you will be subjected to all kinds of lies that tell you that you are not enough. You are not thin enough. You are not tan enough. You are not smooth, soft, shiny, firm, tight, fit, silky, blonde, hairless enough. Your teeth are not white enough. Your legs are not long enough. Your clothes are not stylish enough. You are not educated enough. You don't have enough experience. You are not creative enough.

There is a beauty industry, a fashion industry, a television industry, (and most unfortunately) a pornography industry: and all of these have unique ways of communicating to bright young women: you are not beautiful, smart, or valuable enough.

You must have the clarity and common sense to know that none of that is true. **None of it.**

You were created for a purpose, exactly so. You have innate value. You are loved more than you could ever comprehend; it is mind-boggling how much you are adored. There has never been, and there will never be another you. Therefore, you have unique thoughts to offer the world. They are only yours, and we all lose out if you are too fearful to share them.

You are beautiful. You are valuable. You are enough.

Notes

Chapter One

1. Gerry Goffin, Carole King, and Jerry Wexler, "(You Make Me Feel Like) A Natural Woman," *Tapestry* (Ode Records, 1971).

2. MIT Press Journals, http://www.mitpressjournals. org/doi/abs/10.1162/jocn.2010.21497.

3. C. S. Lewis, *The Weight of Glory* (New York: The Macmillan Company, 1949).

Chapter Two

1. Tweeted by Olivia Wilde, @oliviawilde, May 15, 2011.

2. A thought: A tanning salon would be a great place to run an undercover drug operation. There are so many unidentifiable substances inside that no one would ever be the wiser.

Chapter Three

1. These are real Facebook statuses collected from teenagers I know, however loosely, in 2012. I took the liberty of correcting just enough of the grammatical and spelling errors to make them decipherable.

2. I am making a very dangerous assumption here that she does not have her privacy settings set to "public." If you don't know for sure, go be intrusive and controlling and meddling and all the other terrible things she will say about you and insist that her profiles are set to private. There are a hundred reasons this matters, not the least of which is her safety.

3. Glennon Melton, "Momaquery—On Criticism vs. Cruelty," July 1, 2013, http://momastery.com/blog/2013/07/01/momaquery-on-criticism-vs-cruelty.

Chapter Four

1. See http://www.aniotaoftruth.com/it-is-not-necessary-to-react-to-everything-you-notice.

2. See http://www.goodreads.com/quotes/6463-i-ve-learned-that-you-can-tell-a-lot-about-a.

3. See http://www.aholyexperience.com/2013/06/aletter-to-the-north-american-church-because-it-is-time.

Chapter Five

1. Poe, "Terrified Heart," *Haunted* (Sheridan Square Records, 2000).

2. Stephen Colbert, 2006 White House Correspondents' Dinner, http://politicalhumor.about.com/od/stephencolbert/a/colbertbush.htm.

3. Matt Kirshen, "Homeopathy Is a Crock," *Last Comic Standing*, http://youtu.be/UvH1TnzYch4?t=46s.

4. Dr. Seuss, *Horton Hears a Who* (New York: Random House, 1954).

5. Louie Giglio, http://www.bluefishtv.com/
Store/Downloadable_Video_Illustrations/2280/
Our_Journey__Igniting_Our_Passion.

6. Joyce Brothers, quoted in *Words of Wisdom: More
Good Advice*, ed. William Safire and Leonard Safir (New
York: Fireside, 1990), 199.

Chapter 6

1. See http://www.netplaces.com/parenting-strong-
willed-kids/maintaining-emotional-sobriety/emotions-good-
servants-bad-masters.htm.

2. *Sleepless in Seattle*, directed by Nora Ephron (Tristar
Pictures, 1993).

3. Jeremiah 31:3; Deuteronomy 12:31; John 2:13–
15; Genesis 6:5–6; Matthew 9:36; Judges 2:18; John
11:35; Luke 15:4–6; Isaiah 30:18; Ephesians 4:30–31;
Deuteronomy 4:23–24; Genesis 1:31; 2 Samuel 22:20.

4. See http://www.unh.edu/emotional_intelligence/
EI%20Assets/Reprints...EI%20Proper/EI1990%20
Emotional%20Intelligence.pdf.

5. See http://www.busines-week.com/news/2012-03-
09/nobel-winning-gbowee-tells-american-women-to-get-
angry-1.

6. Tina Fey, *Bossypants* (New York: Little Brown Book
Group, 2011), 3.

7. Dr. Ted Roberts and Diane Roberts, *Sexy Christians:
The Purpose, Power, and Passion of Biblical Intimacy* (Grand
Rapids: Baker Books, 2010), 94.

8. You know, AWANAS. It's like Girl (and Boy) Scouts
for Baptists. You get a vest and a leader, and you receive

badges and like paraphernalia for memorizing verses
of Scripture each week. As an adult I know it as "that
Wednesday night program at which a classroom full of second grade girls try to get me to sign off on their verses after
I feed them every single word of their verse, like they are
little starlets and I'm their director holding the script off-
stage." "For God so . . . LINE! Oh yeah, *loved* the world
that He . . . LINE! Oh yeah, He *gave* His . . . LINE! Oh
yeah, His only *begotten* son that . . . LINE!" Mercy.

9. There are lists all over the Internet along the lines of
"If you're feeling sad, read this verse," but lists never did it
for me. I recommend giving her a passage to read and letting her find a truth herself; it has to resonate with her. The
more context the better; however much you think you can
get away with asking her to read, max that out.

Chapter Seven

1. See http://www.thetruth.com/facts/1-in-3.

Chapter Eight

1. See http://louisem.com/3943/famous-mark-twain
-quotes.

2. As quoted by Rich Brott, *Biblical Principles for
Becoming Debt Free* (Portland, OR: ABC Book Publishing,
2008).

3. See http://www.geonius.com/eliot/quotes.html.

4. K. P. Yohannan, *Revolution in World Missions*
(Carrollton, TX: Gospel for Asia, 2004), 105.

Chapter Nine

1. From a 1996 commencement address to Wellesley College: http://www.huffingtonpost.com/2012/06/26/norah-ephrons-commencement-96-address_n_1628832.html.

2. *Downton Abbey*, PBS 2010, creator Julian Fellowes, season 3, episode 4.

3. Shauna Niequist, *Bittersweet* (Grand Rapids: Zondervan, 2013), 185.

4. John Green, http://www.youtube.com/watch?v=rMweXVWB918, 2009.

5. Amy Poehler, quotes compiled from "Smart Girls at the Party," http://sgatp.net.

Chapter Ten

1. As quoted by Lou Kennedy, *Business Etiquette for the Nineties: Your Ticket to Career Success* (Bluffton, SC: Palmetto Pub., 1992), 8.

2. Quoted by Jim Hightower, *Swim Against the Current, Even a Dead Fish Can Go with the Flow* (Hoboken, NJ: Wiley & Sons, 2008), 3.

3. Jon Foreman, "Let That Be Enough" (re:think Records, 1999).

4. Tina Fey, *Bossypants* (New York: Little Brown Book Group, 2011), 242.

5. Tim Keller, https://twitter.com/timkellernyc/status/345277414273843200.

6. Anne Lamott, *Grace (Eventually): Thoughts on Faith* (New York: Riverhead, 2007), 77.

The world is run by teen girls: parents of teen girls, teachers of teen girls, boys trying to date teen girls, companies trying to sell things to teen girls, and people who have had it "up to here" with teen girls. Chances are, if you're reading this, there is a young woman in your life for whom you desire the very best, and *10 Things for Teen Girls* can help with that.

Rooted in biblical wisdom and interspersed with candid stories of the modern teenage experience, these 10 important truths impart common (and all too uncommon) sense.